Data Protection for Marketers

About the Author

Steven Roberts is a marketer, columnist and author. A certified data protection officer and Fellow of the Chartered Institute of Marketing, he writes regularly for national and international publications on the topics of marketing, strategy and data protection. His articles and commentary have featured in *Business and Finance*, *Business Plus*, the *Irish Examiner*, *Marketing Week*, *Irish Compliance Quarterly* and *Catalyst*. For the past three years, he has contributed a column to *Marketing* magazine.

Steven is head of marketing and data protection lead at Griffith College and sits on its marketing, strategy implementation and GDPR committees. Over the past twenty years he has held senior marketing roles in Ireland and overseas. He is a non-executive director of the Discovery Programme and chair of its communications committee. Steven currently serves as vice-chairperson of the Association of Compliance Officers in Ireland's data protection and information security working group, and was a judge for the 2019 Marketer of the Year Award.

Steven holds a BA (Hons) in History from Trinity College, a MSc in Tourism Management from Technological University Dublin, a Professional Certificate in Date Protection from University College Dublin, a Mini-MBA in Marketing, and a Professional Diploma in Strategy and Innovation from the UCD Michael Smurfit Graduate Business School. He is currently studying for a postgraduate qualification in governance at the Institute of Public Administration.

He is particularly interested in the intersection between marketing, strategy and data privacy.

He lives in Dublin with his wife and two children.

Follow Steven on social media:
LinkedIn: www.linkedin.com/in/stevenroberts-marketing
Twitter: @StevenRoberts1

Data Protection for Marketers

A Practical Guide

STEVEN ROBERTS

ORPEN PRESS

Published by
Orpen Press
Upper Floor, Unit B3
Hume Centre
Hume Avenue
Park West Industrial Estate
Dublin 12

email: info@orpenpress.com
www.orpenpress.com

Paperback ISBN 978-1-78605-098-4
ePub ISBN 978-1-78605-099-1

A catalogue record for this book is available from the British Library.

Printed in Dublin by SPRINTprint Ltd

To Rachael, Ethan and Hope, with love

Acknowledgements

This book is the fulfilment of a long-held ambition. To write something I felt could contribute in a meaningful and helpful way. Written during the pandemic, it was a most welcome distraction from the challenges and upheavals we have all faced in recent months.

I want to thank my wife, Rachael, for her support, without which I could not have completed this book. Her patience and willingness to read through early chapter drafts provided guidance and feedback when it was most needed.

To my editor, Eileen, thank you for your advice and patience as I strove to meet our agreed deadlines. Your insights on everything from cover art to saying more with less have been invaluable.

To my colleagues in Griffith College, the Discovery Programme and the Association of Compliance Officers, thank you for your friendship and ongoing encouragement.

To Michael in *Marketing* magazine, thank you for giving me a platform to share my thoughts on marketing with Irish marketing professionals.

To my parents, Elisabeth and Kevin, with love.

To my sister Kirsten, for your help, advice and deep knowledge of the law.

To my sister Jen, remembered always.

To Ethan and Hope, I hope you like dad's first book!

Contents

1

Introduction

As a profession, marketing is a people-focused industry characterised by fast-paced and multi-disciplinary activity. While no exact figure is available, it is estimated that there are more than 50,000 marketing and communications professionals in Ireland.[1] In the day-to-day life of a marketer, it is not unusual to switch between brand strategy, digital tactics, advertising campaigns and public relations issues, not to mention advising on product and pricing strategy.

Since the turn of the century, marketing has been at the forefront in the adoption of digital technology. Today, there are more than 7,000 marketing technology platforms to choose from.[2] Marketers have been among the main users of social media, search-based advertising and a host of other digital innovations. Fifteen years ago, head of digital and social media manager roles did not exist. Today, they are part of most

---

[1] No exact numbers are available for the Republic of Ireland. The figure of 50,000 is a proportional estimate based on Statista figures for the UK market. D. Clark, 'Total number of sales, marketing and related associate professionals in the United Kingdom (UK) from 2011 to 2020', *Statista*, 4 November 2020, https://www.statista.com/statistics/319805/number-of-sales-marketing-and-related-associate-professionals-in-the-uk/

[2] Scott Brinker, 'Marketing technology landscape supergraphic (2019): Martech 5000 (actually 7,040)', 4 April 2019, https://chiefmartec.com/2019/04/marketing-technology-landscape-supergraphic-2019/

marketing teams. It is clear that as an industry, we have to move fast to keep up with the latest technologies used by our consumers.

In such a busy environment, it is easy to get distracted by tactics and the day-to-day turmoil of a busy professional working life. Indeed, this very issue is at the heart of current debates in marketing on the need to return to strategy and brand building, and away from an obsessive focus on short-term activities. That, however, is for another book.

My aim is to focus marketers' attention on another fundamental issue that has emerged over the past decade – data protection and consumer privacy. There are a number of factors driving increased consumer awareness. First is the introduction, on 25 May 2018, of the European Union's General Data Protection Regulation (GDPR). With potential fines of up to €20 million, or 4 per cent of global turnover, the penalties involved for non-compliant businesses can no longer be ignored. It has also led to a boom in data protection roles; current estimates suggest that up to 75,000 new data protection officers will be needed globally as a result of the introduction of GDPR.[3]

The second key factor is the rise of big technology firms such as Google, Facebook and Twitter. These and other companies have developed a business model for the internet that relies on the trade of individuals' personal data in return for providing 'free' internet and social media platforms. The result is a massive global market in personal data. This market underpins the current advertising technology or adtech model used by marketers across the globe. Capturing consumer data at ever more granular levels, and sharing it with multiple third parties, allows marketers and the businesses they work for to track the behaviours and preferences of billions of individuals globally, all with the intention of providing ever more targeted products and services.

Much of this occurs with little transparency, or understanding on the part of the consumer. Recent scandals such as that surrounding Cambridge Analytica, and questions regarding the involvement of bad actors in national elections have drawn attention to the fundamental privacy implications of this model. As a result, new and proposed data privacy legislation has emerged rapidly over the past 36 months. A recent

[3] Rita Heimes and Sam Pfeifle, 'Study: GDPR's global reach to require at least 75,000 DPOs worldwide', 9 November 2016, IAPP, https://iapp.org/news/a/study-gdprs-global-reach-to-require-at-least-75000-dpos-worldwide

example is the California Consumer Privacy Act (CCPA), which mirrors many aspects of the GDPR and came into effect in 2020.

Marketers can no longer turn a blind eye to the data privacy implications of the adtech model that underpins much of their day-to-day digital marketing activity. Recent reports by two of Europe's leading supervisory authorities, the Information Commissioner's Office (ICO) in the UK[4] and the Commission Nationale Informatique et Libertés (CNIL) in France,[5] have raised very significant questions as to the level of data sharing, the lack of transparency, and adtech's failure to adhere to basic GDPR principles. In addition to the data protection implications, experts such as Dr Johnny Ryan and Dr Augustine Fou have highlighted very substantial issues around cyber-security and fraud.[6]

Finally, rapid advances in robotics, automation and artificial intelligence mean that the use and production of data is going to increase exponentially in the coming years. Machine learning, the internet of things and new technologies such as voice-based search will result in unprecedented levels of data. Consumers are becoming more aware of the trade-offs involved. Products such as Alexa have the potential to provide productivity benefits in the household, but these 'always on' listening devices can also capture the minutiae of a person's daily life. This raises concerns as to what information is being obtained, processed and stored, and how it might be combined with other data sets to which suppliers or third parties may have access.

Marketers are typically some of the largest users of personal data in a firm. Activities such as email campaigns, re-targeting activity, loyalty campaigns and the development of consumer relationship databases all require large volumes of customers' personal data.

As an industry, we tend to be more comfortable with the people-facing aspects of business: communications, events, PR, advertising, etc. Many marketers are happy to leave the minutiae of legal and financial matters

---

[4] Simon McDougall, 'Summary report of adtech Fact Finding Forum, held 6 March 2019', March 2019, https://ico.org.uk/about-the-ico/research-and-reports/adtech-fact-finding-forum

[5] 'Ciblage pulicitaire en ligne: quel plan d'action de la CNIL?', CNIL, 28 June 2019, https://www.cnil.fr/fr/ciblage-publicitaire-en-ligne-quel-plan-daction-de-la-cnil

[6] Johnny Ryan, 'Regulatory complaint concerning massive, web-wide data breach by Google and other "ad tech" companies under Europe's GDPR', *Brave*, 12 September 2018, https://brave.com/adtech-data-breach-complaint/

to other departments. This cannot be the case with personal data. I would argue that it is of fundamental importance that marketers develop a deep understanding of data privacy. It is crucial in their role as the voice of the consumer within their organisation – maintaining and building a trusting relationship – but also as a primary user of data.

Many current data protection texts are primarily written by and intended for the use of privacy, compliance and legal professionals. They contain technical and legalistic terminology that can be off-putting for professionals outside these sectors. For this reason, I felt it necessary to write this book for an audience that has few dedicated privacy textbooks to work from. It is not intended to be a comprehensive overview of every aspect of data protection. Rather, my hope is that by covering the fundamentals, and providing relevant marketing-based examples, it will form the bedrock from which marketers can continue to develop and grow their knowledge.

The world of data protection is changing fast. New legislation is pending, such as the ePrivacy Regulation, which will further alter the privacy ecosystem. Marketers who start the journey today will be well placed to navigate these new developments.

As a Fellow of the Chartered Institute of Marketing with more than 20 years' national and international experience, and as a certified data protection officer, I believe I can bring a unique view to this field, a view that encapsulates the thinking of both sectors.

I hope you enjoy this book. I look forward to a future where many more marketing professionals will see data protection as an important skillset to develop as part of their broader roles.

2

What Is Personal Data?

Chapter 2 at a glance

1. The GDPR covers the personal data of living persons.
2. Personal data includes any information relating to an identified or identifiable natural person.
3. The GDPR applies to processing that is wholly or partly automated, or that forms part of a filing system.
4. Information relating to companies or public bodies is not personal data.

Before we go further, we need to clarify what constitutes personal data. It is a key question. The GDPR's 99 articles relate only to personal data. They do not cover other information that marketers and companies use every day. If you are not processing personal data, then GDPR does not apply.

The GDPR defines personal data as 'any information relating to an identified or identifiable natural person', also known as a data subject.[7] Information on deceased persons is not covered. Article 4(1) of the GDPR

[7] The terms 'consumer', 'customer' and 'data subject' are used interchangeably throughout the book. The terms 'consumer' and 'customer' are more recognisable to marketers.

describes an identifiable individual as one who can be 'identified directly or indirectly'. It provides a range of examples, including:

- A person's name
- An identification number
- Location data
- An online identifier such as a name
- One or more factors specific to the physical, physiological, genetic, mental, economic, cultural or social identity of that natural person

The data must form part of a filing system and/or be wholly or partly processed by automated means.[8] A filing system is structured (for example, by number or alphabetically) and organised in such a way that the information it contains is easily accessed.

Identifying an Individual Indirectly

It is important for marketers to realise that consumers can be distinguished through a combination of data points, each of which would not on its own be sufficient to identify an individual. Together, they can be combined to create a detailed picture of a person. This has relevance to marketing. We capture a wide range of data about our customers through aspects such as programmatic advertising, mobile applications, customer relationship management (CRM) platforms, loyalty programmes, web analytics packages and various types of database.

In 2016, the Court of Justice of the European Union (CJEU) ruled that online IP (internet protocol) addresses could constitute personal data in certain circumstances. IP addresses are like digital fingerprints; they identify a particular computer on a web server. Websites often record and track users' online behaviour for commercial purposes. They may also, on request, disclose records to law enforcement agencies and owners of copyright-protected content. In the CJEU's ruling, a dynamic IP address could be considered personal data if the data controller has the ability to legally add additional information it already had on file.

---

[8] Under GDPR, a filing system is described as 'any structured set of personal data which are accessible according to specific criteria, whether centralised, decentralised or dispersed on a functional or geographic basis'.

It is therefore possible that a set of information held by one firm may not be considered personal data, but it could be for the purposes of another. It depends on the additional data sets to which the firm legally has access.

For example, if a marketing team can merge geolocation and cookie data they may be able to form a detailed, identifiable picture of specific customers. A concert venue's marketers may be able to match mobile data from its publicly accessible Wi-Fi network with information they have on file regarding the individual's financial information or contact details. In reaching an assessment of likelihood, ascertain what could be considered reasonably likely taking account of factors such as cost, time and the technology available. Recital 26 of GDPR advises controllers[9] to consider 'all the means reasonably likely to be used, such as singling out, either by the controller or by another person to identify the natural person directly or indirectly'.

Anonymised and Pseudonymised Data

If data is completely anonymous it does not come under GDPR. However, if another form of encryption has taken place, such as pseudonymisation (a technique where certain identifiers are removed) it can still be considered personal data. Pseudonymised and anonymised data are therefore quite different. The former, however, can still be a very valuable tool in helping reduce privacy risks.

Special Categories of Personal Data

Article 9 of the GDPR identifies special categories of personal data. These data are 'particularly sensitive in relation to fundamental rights and freedoms'. As such, they merit special protection. The following categories of data must therefore meet a higher bar of compliance in order to be processed:

- Personal data revealing an individual's race or ethnicity
- Data relating to a person's political opinions

[9] A data controller is an individual or business that determines the purposes and means of processing. We will look at the various responsibilities and duties of data controllers and processors under GDPR in a later chapter.

- Religious or philosophical beliefs
- Trade union membership
- Genetic data
- Biometric data
- Health data
- Data concerning a person's sex life or sexual orientation

In order to have a legal basis for processing data, one of the following grounds must be met:

1. Explicit consent has been provided by the data subject.
2. It is necessary for the vital interests of the individual, where the person is physically or legally incapable of giving their consent.
3. Specific rights and obligations exist under employment or social welfare law.
4. It is necessary for a medical assessment, diagnosis or treatment.
5. It relates to legal advice or legal proceedings.
6. It is necessary for archiving, research or statistical purposes.
7. It is required for the purposes of providing an insurance, pension or mortgage product.
8. There are substantial public interest reasons. The processing should be proportionate to the aim pursued.
9. It is in the public interest relating to public health. For example, where serious cross-border health threats exist.
10. It relates to the legitimate activity of not-for-profit bodies, as long as appropriate safeguards are in place.
11. The data has already been made public by the individual.

Defining Explicit Consent

Readers may be confused as to the difference between consent and explicit consent. It is still an area of debate among legal and compliance professionals as the GDPR already sets out very clear requirements for consent with regard to personal data.

It appears the ambition of GDPR is to make clear that implied and assumed consent is never possible when dealing with special category data. The UK's ICO states that explicit consent is best advanced when it is 'affirmed in a clear statement (whether oral or written)'.

Why This Is Important for Marketers

Throughout this book, I emphasise the importance of regular training and upskilling in data privacy best practice. A fundamental building block for marketing teams is the ability to identify what is personal data. This provides clarity when responding to time-bound requirements such as the one-month response time for subject access requests. It means that any audit of data held by the marketing department is streamlined to mapping this information. Much time can be wasted collating information, in response to such a request, that turns out not to be directly relevant because it does not fall within the GDPR's definition of personal data.

For companies that handle special category data, it is imperative that marketing teams recognise the higher bar for compliance that is required. There are many businesses for which this will be relevant. For example, a marketing manager of a local gym or health club may have access to health or biometric data. Combining this with other data sets, without recognising their sensitivity under the GDPR, could create significant compliance issues. Similarly, a marketer of a fitness app may be tempted to match this with other personal data held on its clients. While this might result in more complete profiles of its typical customers, the marketer has inadvertently used special category data to build these profiles.

Similarly, there are benefits to recognising when privacy legislation refers specifically to personal data, such as GDPR, and when it refers to the privacy of data more broadly, such as the e-privacy laws. As the national and global privacy landscape becomes more complex in the next few years, making this distinction will become increasingly important.

3

A Brief History of Data Protection

Chapter 3 at a glance

1. Data protection and privacy are separate and distinct rights within the EU's Charter of Fundamental Rights.
2. History and culture play a significant role in how countries approach the issue of data privacy. European countries have played a leading role in the development of data laws.
3. Ireland passed its first privacy law, the Data Protection Act, in 1988.
4. The General Data Protection Regulation (GDPR) is the EU's attempt to provide a consistent level of data protection for EU citizens across all member states.
5. Globally, the introduction of GDPR has led to many other countries and states enhancing their privacy legislation.
6. This is driven by factors such as consumer concerns over data usage and increasing awareness of the downside of a data-driven 'surveillance economy'.

At this point, it is useful for marketers to acquaint themselves with the history and background of data protection and consumer privacy within Europe, particularly Ireland and the UK.

In the European Union (EU) the Charter of Fundamental Rights of the European Union (European Charter) mentions both the right to privacy and the right to data protection. They are viewed as separate and distinct rights. The right to respect for private life is covered in Article 7 of the Charter, while the right to personal data protection is provided for in Article 8.

The Treaty on the Functioning of the European Union and the Treaty on European Union outline the competencies of the European Union in relation to what it can legislate. Data protection law is covered in Article 16(1) of the Treaty on the Functioning of the European Union, which states that 'Everyone has the right to the protection of personal data concerning them'. Article 16(2) states that the EU shall provide data protection rules to uphold this right.

The Importance of History and Culture

It is important to factor in the impact of each EU country's history and culture with regard to data protection. There are considerable differences in how it is viewed. In the Nordic countries, for example, it is not unusual for people to publicly disclose their salaries. Each year Sweden, Finland and Norway publish everyone's income tax returns. In Sweden, anyone can find out their neighbour's salary with a quick phone call to the tax authorities. The person whose returns you request will know it was you, but that is all. The practice dates back to the eighteenth century. In Ireland and Britain, by contrast, one's salary is considered to be very much a private matter; albeit this is breaking down somewhat with younger generations.

Similarly, the experience of living under oppressive, surveillance-based regimes has moulded the views and data protection cultures of Eastern Europeans. Some studies suggest that as many as one in every hundred East Germans were members of the Stasi, the country's secret police during Soviet times.[10] Poland experienced oppression of its nationalist movements in the same period. It is for these reasons that the General

[10] 'East German Stasi had 189,000 informers, study says', *Deutsche Welle*, https://www.dw.com/en/east-german-stasi-had-189000-informers-study-says/a-3184486-1

Data Protection Regulation (GDPR) treats membership of a trade union as particularly sensitive data, but does not place a person's financial data on the same level.

The European approach to data protection has tended to contrast with those of other jurisdictions. The United States, for example, has typically adopted a more liberal attitude to the use of personal data. Its entrepreneurial and individualistic culture appears more favourable to the trade-off involved in sharing increasing amounts of personal information in return for free or highly personalised products and services.

Global attitudes to personal privacy have, however, shifted substantially in recent years. In the USA at present, there is ongoing debate and lobbying at both federal and state level for increased data protection legislation. One such example is the California Consumer Privacy Act. Passed in mid-2018, the Act came into effect on 1 January 2020 and seeks to mirror many aspects of GDPR. In the intervening period, other states, including Nevada and Maine, have also introduced new laws in this area.

Data Protection Law in Europe

Sweden was the first country in the world to introduce a national data protection law (Datalagen), doing so on 11 May 1973. Ireland's first privacy law was the Data Protection Act 1988. The Irish Office of the Data Protection Commissioner was established in 1989.

In Britain, the Data Protection Act 1984 was followed by the Access to Personal Files Act of 1987. This was updated in 1998 with the passing of a new Data Protection Act.

The first piece of EU legislation specifically covering data protection was EU Directive 95/46. It came into force on 24 October 1995. As a directive, it was open to each member state to adopt it into their national laws. This resulted in significant differences of interpretation and anomalies across the EU, something which the GDPR has since sought to rectify.

Legislation has continued to develop in the intervening years. Ireland and Britain both introduced new Data Protection Acts in 2018 to take account of GDPR. As the GDPR is a regulation rather than a directive, it was required to be transposed directly into each country's national law, with very little room for interpretation or derogations.

Digital Single Market

Data privacy law also takes account of broader economic and societal trends. In 2015, the EU outlined its vision for a digital single market (DSM). At its core, the DSM seeks to ensure the free movement of persons, services and capital, with the result that businesses can access online services fairly. This will allow Europe to maximise the growth potential of its digital economy by removing potential barriers for consumers and businesses. The document places a heavy emphasis on high levels of consumer and personal data protection, irrespective of which EU member state a citizen resides in. This is seen as key to ensuring that EU citizens have trust in the single market.

The DSM is founded on three pillars:

1. Better access for consumers and businesses to online goods and services across Europe
2. Creating the right conditions for digital networks and services to flourish
3. Maximising the growth potential of the European digital economy

The GDPR, and upcoming laws such as the ePrivacy Regulation, are fundamental components of this vision for a digital single market. The DSM is also driving related legislation and member states' strategies in adjacent areas such as cyber-security and artificial intelligence.

Consumer Concerns

While political efforts to improve trading conditions have made a contribution, much of the momentum for these changes has arisen from increased consumer concern around the use of personal data. Scandals such as Cambridge Analytica and a series of large-scale data breaches at high-profile companies including Marriott International and British Airways has led many citizens to question just why, where and how their data is being used.

This has also prompted a response from the media. A range of publications, films and documentaries have been produced seeking to give the public a greater understanding of the importance of data in the modern economy. In many ways, data is the new oil, a fundamental building block of the twenty-first-century global economy. Academic and author Shoshana Zuboff's recent best-selling book *The Age of Surveillance Capitalism* appears to have captured much of these concerns. Futurist Yuval Noah Harari has spoken of his concerns regarding increasingly powerful artificial intelligence technologies. In 2019, Netflix released the film *The Great Hack*, documenting the Cambridge Analytica scandal, while the *New York Times* ran a series of articles, opinion and investigative pieces under the title *The Privacy Project*.

Why This Is Important for Marketers

For marketers, particularly those with a global or multinational remit, consumer concerns and the new laws these concerns have generated have significantly increased the level of complexity required to ensure that marketing activity and data usage remain compliant. The risks of non-compliance are substantial. Alongside significant potential fines, perhaps the greater threat is the impact such negative coverage will have on consumer trust and the company's brand reputation. Once damaged, these are not easily fixed.

It is also important to recognise that while efforts are under way in certain jurisdictions, such as the EU, to harmonise laws, significant differences remain. In some cases, these are becoming more divergent. For example, in the USA states respond with privacy bills in the absence of a federal law.

Business-to-business marketers operating across the UK, Ireland and Germany, for instance, will need to take account of the different approaches to contacting potential new clients. Ireland and the UK typically take a more laissez-faire approach, allowing these contacts to be communicated to but with the option to opt out, than Germany and the Netherlands, which require an opt-in for such marketing activity to be compliant.

Culture and history play a substantial part in how any laws are interpreted. New legislation sits atop, and reflects, the ethics, morals and heritage of a particular country. Many businesses will look to international opportunities for growth in the coming years, as we emerge from the impact of the Covid-19 pandemic. As professionals charged with being the voice of the customer inside the firm, and the voice of the company to the outside world, marketers with an international remit must keep such an understanding uppermost in their minds.

4

Data Protection Principles

Chapter 4 at a glance

1. GDPR is based on data protection principles and is technology neutral.
2. These principles form the backbone of GDPR. It is crucial that all members of a marketing team have a good understanding of them.
3. The overarching principle of accountability is fundamental to GDPR.
4. To provide clarity and transparency, marketers should ensure that privacy statements, retention policies and other related data protection information are written in easy-to-understand, straightforward language.
5. Relevant privacy information should be included on any offline data capture forms.

Data protection principles lie at the core of GDPR. They are neutral in that they do not set out legal requirements for specific contexts or technologies. This allows EU member states to respond quickly to the rapid changes experienced in the economy and broader culture. For example, consumers and industry are still coming to terms with new technologies such as artificial intelligence, blockchain, machine learning and facial recognition software. Having a thorough understanding of each of the main principles helps marketing teams as they seek to be compliant in their day-to-day activities.

This chapter looks at each principle in detail and provides examples for marketers as to how they can consider and apply them. As part of this, we will look at the overarching requirement of accountability. This is the obligation for businesses to be cognisant of privacy and to embed it in a transparent and documented manner in all their undertakings. Though mentioned sparsely in the Regulation text, accountability is part of the core ethos of GDPR.

Lawful, Fair and Transparent Processing of Personal Data

Any processing of consumers' personal data must first be lawful. To meet this requirement, marketers must ensure that processing aligns with one of the six legal bases.

Consideration should be given at the outset as to whether the activity meets one of the following:

- Affirmative consent received from the individual in advance
- For the purposes of a contract
- For public interest reasons
- If it is in the vital interest of the data subject
- If a requirement exists under law
- If the company has a legitimate interest (that is not overridden by the rights of the consumer)

Marketers should give due time to this process. For example, if you opt for consent as your legal basis, remember that the consumer can withdraw it at any time. This may create issues if you base your marketing activity on the assumption of continued, ongoing contact with the customer.

To meet the requirements for fairness and transparency, it must be clear to the data subject at the outset what information you will capture, and for what purpose. Too many website privacy notices, for example, still use legal jargon and confusing text that leave customers unclear on both of these aspects. Take the time to ensure that such statements and other related data protection information are concise, transparent and written in plain, straightforward language. It should not require a legal or compliance background to understand them; they must be intelligible to the average member of the public.

When collecting or recording data, provide consumers with relevant information including the identity of the organisation, the contact details of the data protection officer, the purposes and legal bases for data collection, whom the information will be disclosed to or processed by, and the retention periods for the data.

Privacy information extends beyond a notice on your website. For example, most marketers still use data capture forms at fairs, workshops and other promotional events. Relevant data protection information should be included on these forms, so that customers and prospects are clear as to how their data is being processed.

Purpose Limitation

When collecting and processing personal data, marketers must be very clear at the time of collection as to the specific purpose for which the data will be used. These purposes should be set out in the firm's privacy notice.

In the event that you wish to undertake further processing that is not compatible with the original purpose, the data subjects must be informed prior to any new processing taking place. As described by the Information Commissioner's Office in the UK: 'You can only use the personal data for a new purpose if either this is compatible with your original purpose, you get consent, or you have a clear obligation or function set out in law.'

Marketers must also avoid linking purposes together. If a mobile company is using data for essential purposes, such as processing bank account and address details when setting up a new customer account, the consumer must have the option to opt out of any proposed non-essential use such as marketing. This is described by GDPR as processing *in a manner that is incompatible with those purposes*.[11]

There are some exemptions to purpose limitation; however, they are unlikely to be relevant to the vast majority of marketing activity. These are:

- Archiving in the public interest
- For the purposes of scientific or historical research
- For statistical purposes

[11] GDPR Article 5(1)(b).

Data Minimisation

Many marketers have traditionally taken the view that if they are undertaking a data capture activity, it is best to obtain as much information as possible. The primary drivers appear to be efficiency (not having to go out to the market again); perceived value for money; and a sense that more information is always a good thing.

The GDPR challenges this assumption. A key principle of the Regulation is the concept of data minimisation. It advises that any processing of personal data must be adequate to the specific needs involved, be relevant, and limited to only what is necessary for the particular purpose for which they've been obtained. The processing should only take place if it cannot be undertaken reasonably by other means.

This requires a fundamental mind-shift on the part of marketing and communication professionals. For example, a marketing manager running a data capture campaign at an event may choose to collect information on a person's name, address, email, age category, and behavioural or psychographic interests. However, if this is purely for the purpose of sending them a newsletter, the manager should consider reducing collection to just the name and email details. It would be difficult to justify a legitimate basis for capturing the additional information. If these details were to be used for another purpose, the marketer would need to identify this at the time of obtaining the data.

I would argue that data minimisation is beneficial to marketers, for the following reasons:

- It makes compliance easier to achieve.
- It ensures that focus and consideration is given to any data gathering.
- It prevents the storage of large volumes of irrelevant data on the basis that it might be of use in the future.
- Most important, it reduces the potential exposure of the marketing team. The more data held, the more issues may arise with regard to retention and possible breaches.

Marketers should therefore work on the basis of 'If you don't need it, don't collect it.'

Data Accuracy

The next principle, accuracy, segues nicely from our discussion on data minimisation. If a marketing team holds personal data, it is obliged to ensure that the data is accurate and up to date. If the data remains relevant, within retention timelines, and is still being used for its original purpose, marketers must take all reasonable steps to ensure that it contains no inaccuracies. On finding any errors, every effort should be made to correct these in a timely manner, either through erasure or rectification, whichever is most appropriate in the particular case.

Apart from its importance for overall business and marketing efficacy, having accurate data will also be vital in the context of subject access requests (SARs). These can be made at any stage by customers or other stakeholders for whom your team or business holds personal data. Recent widespread coverage of GDPR, and increased consumer interest and concerns regarding their privacy, mean that we are likely to see more SARs in the future.

Consumers are entitled to rectification and the prompt correction of any errors that may be identified when they are sent their personal data. Article 16 of the GDPR states:

> ***The data subject shall have the right to obtain from the controller without undue delay the rectification of inaccurate personal data concerning him or her. Taking into account the purposes of the processing, the data subject shall have the right to have incomplete personal data completed, including by means of providing a supplementary statement.***

It is therefore key that processes are in place to update any personal data in a prompt and timely manner once notifications of amendments are received.

Storage Limitation

Do not keep personal data for longer than needed. Article 5(1)(e) of the GDPR states that data controllers are required to store personal data for no longer than is necessary for the purposes for which it was originally collected.

Key to this is ensuring that your organisation has a clear data retention policy. This states how long the company or department retains specific types of personal data. It also outlines the rationale for keeping data for that time period. In the run-up to GDPR, many companies' compliance teams spent significant time reviewing and updating their retention policies.

There are several considerations to take into account. For instance, are there legal or regulatory standards that require the data to be held for a particular period of time? Examples might include employment law and information needed for income tax and auditing purposes.

For particular industries, there may be guidelines in place that are standard for those sectors. While they do not guarantee compliance, they can provide useful guidance when establishing or updating your marketing team's retention policies.

The GDPR does not state specific retention periods. Instead, it relies on each controller to evaluate and justify the timelines based on the legal bases being utilised and the purposes for which the data is being processed.

As a general rule, storage limitation promotes efficiency. Marketers hold on to less unnecessary data, with lower related storage and data maintenance costs; and it facilitates swifter responses to subject access requests (SARs). Remember, you are legally obliged to provide the data subject with all personal data currently on file. So the more information you retain, the more you are mandated to peruse and collate when responding to a SAR. This can be important when endeavouring to meet the 30-day response limit under GDPR.

Data deletion at the end of a retention period also requires careful consideration. The firm may have a legitimate interest in retaining some information, for example when a customer requests that they no longer receive promotional information from the business. It is reasonable for that company to hold on to sufficient information, even after the customer stops using its service, to ensure that they do not receive any future direct marketing communications.

There are a few exemptions to the storage limitation requirements; specifically, where the data is used for public interest archiving, scientific or historical research, or for statistical purposes.

Integrity and Confidentiality

When you obtain or process personal data, the GDPR places a legal requirement on you to ensure that its integrity and confidentiality is maintained for as long as you retain it. Marketers, as one of the main users of personal data, must have appropriate technical and security measures in place. It is also a key requirement when considering the introduction of new marketing or technology platforms that utilise personal data.

It is worth remembering also that integrity and confidentiality cover a wide range of aspects, including protection against unauthorised or unlawful processing and against accidental loss, destruction or damage. It should take into account what could be considered reasonable, given the size and resources of the firm, the type of data being stored, and the scale of processing being undertaken by the business.

One of the most important aspects to assess is the user rights provided to access the data. How often are these reviewed and updated to reflect changes in your team? And what levels of access does each team member need? In 2019, the Data Protection Commissioner Helen Dixon advised that the majority of data breaches reported to her office involved some level of human error.[12] Alongside training, it is therefore key to have a clear user access policy for your firm's marketing platforms. In most businesses, this can be achieved in conjunction with the company's IT or compliance teams.

Accountability

Accountability, the overarching theme of the GDPR, is regularly identified as the seventh data protection principle. Article 5(2) states that 'the controller shall be responsible for, and be able to demonstrate compliance with, [the principles listed in] paragraph 1 ("accountability").'

In a nutshell, accountability is about embedding data protection principles throughout one's organisation, placing data privacy at the heart of the business. In that sense, it is the responsibility of every single person within the business – from the marketing director, CEO and board to frontline and operational staff.

---

[12] Peter Hamilton, 'Data commissioner to look for more staff and funding', *Irish Times*, 7 March 2019, https://www.irishtimes.com/business/technology/data-commissioner-to-look-for-more-staff-and-funding-1.3817791

From a practical perspective, it means that marketing teams and the businesses they work for should be able to demonstrate to the Data Protection Commission, their customers and other stakeholders that they are compliant and meeting all their obligations under the Regulation.

Key to this is documentation. In the event of a breach, data protection supervisory authorities are far more likely to be understanding if documentation, policies and controls are in place; and, more important, if these are living documents that are shared and understood across the organisation, and updated on a regular basis. Documentation, however, is not sufficient on its own. A marketing team must be able to demonstrate that the principle of accountability is being adhered to in the regular day-to-day life of the business.

For example, a team might consider introducing a new customer relationship management (CRM) system to improve its ability to communicate effectively with customers and potential clients. One way in which the team can demonstrate compliance with the accountability principle is to show that they have assessed the potential data protection implications of the platform. This could be achieved by undertaking an initial data protection impact assessment (DPIA), to assess whether a full DPIA is required, and to document any mitigating actions that are needed to maximise the data privacy and security of the consumers' data on the new system.

When GDPR came into force, many businesses struggled to understand how best to demonstrate accountability. It can be difficult to know where to start. One practical approach is to develop an overall document or framework that acts as the hub for recording all elements of your firm's data protection compliance. Another important step is proactively monitoring your policies and procedures to ensure that they continue to be effective.

Training and development form a crucial component. Rather than running a once-off training session for your marketing staff, make sure to regularly revisit their data protection needs. This could be in the form of encouraging attendance at GDPR workshops – many legal firms offer regular talks and seminars in this area. Another method might be a yearly or half-yearly workshop. This gives members a chance to raise any data protection issues or incidents that have arisen in the preceding months. Consider identifying a champion within the team; someone who is either a regular point person with your legal and compliance departments, or who has the task of monitoring the environment on a reasonably regular basis and circulating updates to colleagues. This could be as simple as checking in weekly or fortnightly with sites such as the Data Protection Commissioner or the International Association of Privacy Professionals (IAPP).[13]

Why This Is Important for Marketers

The GDPR consists of 99 Articles. Few, if any, are more important than Article 5. To know the principles underlying the Regulation is to have a fundamental understanding of what is and is not compliant. It is one of the first places marketers should start when getting to grips with data protection.

A few examples should be sufficient to give a sense of their importance.

1. A marketing team aware that any use of data must be lawful will know that they need to consider which of the six legal bases a new project or activity will rely upon.
2. A manager who understands the principle of data minimisation will question his or her team as to whether a new mobile app needs to capture such a wide array of customers' data.
3. A business owner schooled in the principle of storage limitation will ensure that there are clear data retention policies in place across the company.
4. A chief marketing officer who understands the importance of accountability will ensure that their team is aware of the need to document their activity and have clear processes in place for how personal data is obtained and processed.

Having a good knowledge of these principles gives a marketing team something intangible but highly valuable – confidence. Few outside legal and compliance specialists will have a complete understanding of the GDPR, but knowing and applying the GDPR principles provides marketers with the assurance that they are looking after the needs of their business

[13] These can be found at www.dataprotection.ie and www.iapp.org. Both are excellent sources of information on the latest trends, updates and changes in the data privacy landscape, with the IAPP website taking a more global view of privacy.

and their customers. It gives them the self-belief to challenge practices across the organisation that may be non-compliant or ill-considered – in other words, to act as champions for data privacy. In doing so, they will also act as champions for the trust and reputation of the brands they manage.

5

The Lawful Bases for Processing Personal Data

Chapter 5 at a glance

1. The lawful bases for processing personal data are a fundamental element of GDPR compliance.
2. The accountability principle requires marketers to keep clear records of the lawful basis under which processing has taken place.
3. Marketers will usually rely on consent, contract or legitimate interest.
4. Consent must be freely given, specific, informed and unambiguous. It must be as easy to withdraw consent as it was to provide it in the first place.
5. When considering legitimate interests as a lawful basis, it is worth undertaking a legitimate interests assessment (LIA) to ensure that the processing is necessary, proportionate and balances the rights of the individual with the interests of the firm.
6. When considering further processing of data, marketers should reflect on how the consumer would reasonably expect their data to be used.

Marketers need to be familiar with the lawful bases upon which they can process personal data. These lie at the core of GDPR compliance. Familiarity with them is one of the foundation stones of an effective data protection culture. Article 6 of the Regulation[14] outlines six legal bases for processing personal information. All processing must fall within one of these areas:

1. Consent has been given by the data subject.
2. It is required for the performance of a contract.
3. It is required under law.
4. It is in the vital interests of the data subject.
5. It is in the public interest.
6. A legitimate interest exists, except where such interests are overridden by the rights of the data subject.

Marketers are most likely to use consent, contract or legitimate business interest in their day-to-day activities; however, it is useful to have a clear understanding of all six bases. The individual's right to be informed under Articles 13 and 14 of the GDPR means that this information will need to be included in your company's privacy notice.

Before deciding which basis is most appropriate, a marketer must first understand the reason for the data processing taking place. Which one of the above legal bases is most relevant? Taking time at the outset to be 100 per cent clear on this rationale is important as it reduces the risk of non-compliance or exposure at a later stage.

Consent

Consent is the legal basis with which many marketers are most familiar. Any of us operating e-newsletter mailing lists, for example, will be aware of the need to have an affirmative opt-in from each individual before sending marketing-related information to them.

The GDPR is very clear on what constitutes consent. It must be 'freely given, specific, informed and unambiguous'.[15] The person must give their consent via a 'statement or by a clear affirmative action' agreeing to the

14 Regulation (EU) 2016/679, hereafter referred to as the GDPR.

15 Article 4(11) GDPR.

processing of personal data relating to him or her. To explore the topic in more detail, we will break down each of these phrases.

Freely Given

The term 'freely given' is an important one. It ensures that no duress is placed on the data subject. This includes situations where there could be a potential imbalance of power, for example in a company setting where the employer requests consent from one of its employees to use his or her personal data. Given the employer's position as paymaster, this would be perceived as having undue influence on the employee's decision.

The GDPR is clear: 'Consent should not be regarded as freely given if the data subject has no genuine or free choice or is unable to refuse or withdraw consent without detriment.'[16]

In a marketing context, consider a situation where a website requires consumers to consent to their data being shared with third-party providers before they can read the website's content. This form of 'cookie wall' reduces the visitor's ability to make a free choice. It is not in keeping with the spirit of the GDPR. The issue of cookie walls is also being reviewed as part of the forthcoming ePrivacy Regulation, something we will cover in more detail in later chapters.

Specific

Consent must relate specifically to the processing that will take place. Marketers should not combine separate processing requests, for example, to join a mailing list from a company and also to join a separate mailing list for third-party firms. In a scenario where consent is being sought for two separate activities, this must be clearly specified. In this instance, the data subject should have the option to consent to both lists, to join one of the two, or to join neither list.

Informed

In order for a consumer to be informed, the GDPR requires they are aware of the following aspects, expressed in clear and plain language:[17]

---

16 Recital 42 GDPR.

17 Recitals 42 and 43 GDPR.

1. The controller's identity
2. The purpose for which the data has been obtained
3. The data that will be collected
4. The existence of the right to withdraw consent
5. If the data will be utilised for purposes of automated decision-making
6. Whether the data will be transferred outside the EU and, in that instance, what safeguards are in place

When seeking to inform the data subject, marketers must make sure that what they are consenting to is clear. It cannot be buried or hidden within a larger document or across multiple clauses and paragraphs. The information should be able to be reasonably understood by a layperson and it should not include technical terminology or legal jargon.

Unambiguous

Consent cannot be implied or assumed. Many of us will be familiar with websites containing pre-ticked boxes. This use of nudge theory, relying on the data subject's inertia or unwillingness to read what they are signing to push them towards a particular choice, is prohibited under GDPR.

In preparing for the introduction of the Regulation, the removal of implied consent caused significant headaches for many marketers. They feared that databases would be substantially reduced in scale.[18] In hindsight, having fewer contacts, but knowing that those people have freely chosen to receive information on one's product or service, is infinitely preferable to having a large database of cold (or even hostile) contacts, which provided little economic benefit to most businesses and caused significant inefficiencies.

Accountability

Under the GDPR's accountability principle, marketers must be able to demonstrate that they have consent.[19] Record-keeping is therefore vital to ensure that you and your teams can provide clear proof consent has been freely given for a specific form of data processing.

---

[18] Morag Cudderford-Jones, 'How small business are tackling GDPR', *Marketing Week*, 11 April 2018, https://www.marketingweek.com/gdpr-small-businesses/

[19] Articles 5 and 24, and Recitals 39 and 74 GDPR.

Consent can be withdrawn at any stage. This withdrawal should be as easy for the consumer as it was to opt in originally.[20] For that reason, it may be prudent to consider other legal bases that form a longer-lasting, stronger connection. One example is a contract.

Contract

Processing personal data can be compliant with GDPR if it is necessary for the establishment or performance of a contract. For example, a mobile phone operator may need to process a customer's name, email address, bank account details and other relevant information in order to provide its service and to be able to bill him or her monthly as per the terms of a signed contract.

The key word here is 'necessity'. There has to be a clear and necessary reason for the processing to take place as part of the contract. If the business wishes to obtain or process additional data that is not strictly necessary under the contract, another legal basis would have to be found. For example, seeking the customer's consent to receive a monthly newsletter with updates on new products, services or special offers. This is particularly important where the product or service being promoted differs substantially from what the customer has purchased.

Legal Obligation

In some cases, the controller will be subject to a legal requirement to process personal data. Article 6(1)(c) of the GDPR provides a lawful basis where 'processing is necessary for compliance with a legal obligation to which the controller is subject'. The legal obligation must be set down by either Irish or EU law.

For example, a marketing company hires a social media manager. As an employer, it needs to process the new manager's personal data to comply with a legal obligation to disclose employee salary details to the Revenue Commissioners.

As a marketer, you must be able to identify the specific legal provision. Keeping in mind the accountability principle, you should document your decision to rely on this lawful basis and ensure that the rationale for

[20] Article 7(3) GDPR.

the decision can be justified. Seek advice if necessary and work with your legal and compliance teams to ascertain whether your firm can reasonably comply with the legal requirement without having to process personal data.

Vital Interests

Vital interests cover scenarios where processing is required to protect a person's life. Again, this must be necessary. Recital 46 of the GDPR provides some useful guidance: 'Processing of personal data based on the vital interest of another natural person should in principle take place only where the processing cannot be manifestly based on another legal basis.'[21]

Therefore, if it is feasible to protect the individual's life without having to process their personal data, this basis would not apply. It is not possible to rely on vital interests for health or biometric data if the individual is in a position to give or refuse consent.

Public Interest

The GDPR provides a public interest legal basis where 'processing is necessary for the performance of a task carried out in the public interest or in the exercise of official authority vested in the controller.'[22]

This legal basis is most relevant to public authorities, and processing in this manner must have a clear basis in law. It is no longer possible for public authorities to rely upon legitimate interests for this form of processing.

As with all aspects of GDPR, the processing must be proportionate. If the public body or official can find a less intrusive method to achieve the same result, they should do so, ensuring that any processing is adequate and not excessive.

Legitimate Interest

Businesses can claim a legitimate interest in processing consumers' personal data. When using this option, they must ensure that it does not override the rights of the affected individuals. There should be a

21 Recital 46 GDPR.

22 Article 6(1)(e) GDPR.

reasonable expectation on the part of the customer that such activity might take place.

It is worth taking time to consider this aspect in some detail. Many marketers will be faced with scenarios where they must make a reasonable assessment as to whether a legitimate interest exists.

The GDPR advises that a lawful basis exists where 'Processing is necessary for the purposes of the legitimate interests pursued by the controller or by a third party, except where such interests are overridden by the interests or fundamental rights and freedoms of the data subject which require protection of personal data, in particular where the data subject is a child.'[23]

Legitimate interest is one of the most contentious legal bases on which to assume compliance. It is the most flexible lawful basis for processing, but GDPR case law is still in its infancy and there is a certain lack of clarity as to its scope. The Information Commissioner's Office, the UK's data protection supervisory authority, puts it well: 'if you choose to rely on legitimate interests, you are taking on extra responsibility for considering and protecting people's rights and interests.'[24]

Marketers can undertake a legitimate interest assessment (LIA) to examine if this is the most appropriate basis for processing. An LIA considers three elements:

1. Purpose: Does a clear legitimate interest exist for the marketer's company?
2. Necessity: Can it be demonstrated that the processing is necessary to achieve this?
3. Balance: Does it effectively balance the rights and freedoms of data subjects who will be affected by the processing?

The processing must be necessary to achieve the required business result. If this can be arrived at by another method that either requires less data processing or avoids the need to process personal data altogether, then a lawful basis no longer exists.

---

23 Article 6(1)(f) GDPR.

24 'Legitimate interests', ICO, https://ico.org.uk/for-organisations/guide-to-data-protection/guide-to-the-general-data-protection-regulation-gdpr/lawful-basis-for-processing/legitimate-interests/

A business must include information in its privacy statement about how it relies upon legitimate interests for processing data. Under the accountability principle, marketers must also keep a record of any legitimate interest assessments. This enables the business to demonstrate its compliance with GDPR if required by the Data Protection Commission or other relevant supervisory authorities.

As an example, consider a schools liaison officer (SLO) at a third-level university. She wishes to send an email to secondary school guidance counsellors notifying them of an upcoming open day. The SLO's database of contacts does not contain specific confirmation that consent has been provided by these counsellors to receive such mailings. Using the balancing assessment, we can see if a legitimate interest exists.

1. Purpose: There is a legitimate interest in a schools liaison officer providing this information to guidance counsellors. It can be reasonably argued that the recipients will find it useful when giving advice and guidance to students as to their third-level course options.
2. Necessity: With hundreds of guidance counsellors to be contacted, it would be difficult to achieve this communication in a timely manner through other channels such as face to face or via the telephone.
3. Balance: The SLO can reasonably assume an expectation on the part of guidance counsellors that they would receive this information from colleges and universities, and that it would be helpful in the course of their day-to-day activities. If the SLO includes an unsubscribe option with the email, any counsellors wishing to opt out of future communications with the university can do so. This makes withdrawing consent easy and comprehensive for the counsellors as data subjects.

The GDPR advises that direct marketing, such as in a business-to-business situation or the example outlined above, can be considered lawful if there is a reasonable expectation on the part of the recipient that they would be sent such information.[25] The UK and Ireland have traditionally adopted a more liberal approach to business-to-business communications of this sort than other northern European countries such as Germany and the Netherlands. It is worth remembering that individuals retain the

25 Recital 47 GDPR.

right to object to processing used for direct marketing purposes, regardless of the legal basis that is being relied upon.

Particular attention should be paid to scenarios where children's personal data is being processed. Marketing firms that promote products or services to minors must be very mindful of this when undertaking any legitimate interest assessment.

Further Processing

In some cases, the purposes of processing may change over a period of time, or a new purpose may emerge. This may still be lawful as long as it is compatible with the original purpose.

Taking the approach of what could reasonably be expected by the consumer, if the new processing is substantially different it would be prudent for marketers to identify and record the lawful basis involved for this new activity. This aligns with the purpose limitation principle, as outlined in Article 5 of the GDPR. Marketers who are unsure should always ask the question, 'Will this adhere to the requirements of lawfulness, fairness and transparency?' When in doubt, seek advice from your legal counsel, compliance team and data protection officer.

Further processing does not apply in the case of consent. As we saw above, consent must always be specific and informed. In those cases, you may need to re-seek consent from the data subjects, or consider whether a different legal basis may be more appropriate.

It should also be noted that further processing for scientific purposes, archiving in the public interest and processing for statistical purposes are all considered lawful under Article 89(1) of the GDPR. The Data Protection Act 2018 states that additional compatible purposes may include: preventing a threat to national security; preventing, detecting, investigating or prosecuting criminal offences; and for the purposes of seeking or obtaining legal advice.

The GDPR sets a higher bar on processing certain types of special category personal data, for example data relating to a person's health, sex life or political opinions.

Why This Is Important for Marketers

The legal bases for processing personal data are a key pillar of the GDPR. Along with the seven principles, they are absolutely fundamental to an effective understanding of data protection best practice. Businesses looking to train up their teams must ensure that adequate time is spent on each legal basis. It should also form a core part of any refresher training for existing staff.

While marketers may rely primarily on consent, contract or legitimate interest, it is important to be aware of all six legal bases. We are one of the most significant users of data in a firm. It is easy, in the context of demanding targets and a hectic work schedule, to fail to recognise when the purposes of data processing have shifted or, similarly, to fail to devote sufficient time to keep adequate records of LIAs, consumer consent, and other requirements under the accountability principle.

A thorough understanding of this aspect of GDPR reduces such risks. It encourages each marketer to consider at the outset whether there is a lawful rationale for a new campaign or promotional activity. In doing so, they substantially improve the chances of an effective compliance culture taking hold within the business.

6

Data Subjects' Rights

Chapter 6 at a glance

1. Consumers have an expanded set of data protection rights under the GDPR.
2. While not absolute, these rights offer significant additional protections for EU data subjects.
3. At their core, they seek to provide increased levels of trust, control, access and transparency around the use of personal data.
4. Marketing teams must be aware of these rights.
5. In particular, the right of access is likely to be used increasingly by consumers seeking to find out more about how their personal data is being utilised for marketing purposes.
6. Companies that fail to put in place adequate procedures may breach mandatory timelines to respond to requests.

Under GDPR, consumers have an expanded set of data protection rights. The aim is to provide them with greater transparency, control and access to their data, ensuring that data subjects have clarity and trust in how their data is used, the purpose it is being used for, and the knowledge that any information kept for specific purposes is both accurate and up to date. These rights are a fundamental building block of the EU's digital single market strategy. In this chapter, we will look at each of the rights in detail and outline how marketers and the firms they work for can best respond and ensure compliance. It is useful to remember that these rights are not absolute and must be balanced with other rights and legal requirements.

Right of Access

Perhaps the best known of the GDPR rights is the right of access. Under Article 15, individuals have the right to access and obtain a copy of their personal data. In addition, the data subject can request information regarding how the data is being processed and used.[26] This includes aspects such as:

1. The purposes for which the data is being processed
2. The categories of personal data held
3. The recipients or categories of recipient of the personal data; in particular, recipients in third countries or international organisations
4. How long the data will be stored for
5. The right to request that the controller rectify, erase or restrict processing
6. The right to lodge a complaint with a supervisory authority
7. If the data was not collected directly from the individual, information as to its source
8. Whether automated decision-making or profiling is taking place
9. Where personal data is transferred to a third country or to an international organisation, the data subject shall have the right to be informed of the appropriate safeguards relating to the transfer

The GDPR does not stipulate a specific method for making a valid access request. It can be made in writing or orally. The DPC recommends making written requests where possible, to provide clarity for the organisation and a paper trail or record for the individual making the request. In some instances, it may be useful to provide a standard form on your website. Recital 59 of the GDPR advises businesses to 'provide means for requests to be made electronically, especially where personal data are processed by electronic means'.

---

[26] The Data Protection Commission provides a useful FAQ section on its website at https://www.dataprotection.ie/en/dpc-guidance/data-subject-access-requests-faq

Responding to Access Requests

Article 12 of GDPR outlines a number of requirements that businesses must keep top of mind.

First, the timeframe for responding is stated in the Regulation. On receiving a request, businesses have one month to respond. This can be extended by a further two months, where necessary, taking into account the 'complexity and number of the requests'. Where such an extension is required, the data subject must be informed of the delay and the reasons for it. If the business has doubts about the person's identity, it is within its rights to request additional information. However, this should be proportionate to the request being made, and should not be unduly burdensome.

The organisation can refuse to comply under certain circumstances, for example if it believes the request to be frivolous. It must let the individual know without undue delay, and at the latest within one month of receiving the request. When a request is made electronically, the information should be provided by electronic means, unless otherwise requested by the data subject.

Organisations cannot charge a fee for processing the request. According to Article 12(5) of GDPR, information provided under Articles 13 and 14 and relating to the rights under Articles 15 to 22 'shall be provided free of charge'.

The only exception is where the business believes a request to be unfounded, and needs to cover administration costs. An example is where repeated requests are made by a data subject, within a short time period. Context is important. If the company processes large volumes of data on a daily or weekly basis, it may be reasonable for a person to submit frequent requests.

Can I Ask for More Specifics?

It is reasonable and prudent to request clarification on what data is being sought. For example, if a request comes in for 'all my personal data that you have on file', it is fair for the company to ask for more specifics to help it source the information. This could be as simple as providing specific dates. If the data subject fails to provide this, the company must still make all reasonable efforts to provide the information it has to hand. Asking for details cannot be used to avoid or delay the request.

Be Clear on Timelines

There is confusion in many businesses regarding the precise response timeline. Some people consider it to be one month; others interpret it as 30 days. Given that some months are shorter than others, it is useful to provide clarity. The Information Commissioner's Office in the UK provides sensible advice: 'you should calculate the time limit from the day you receive the request (whether it is a working day or not) until the corresponding calendar date in the next month.'[27] If that date falls on a weekend or a public holiday, you have until the next working day after that to respond. If the following month is shorter, the last date for response is the last day of that month. For example, if your business receives an access request on 31 March, you have until 30 of April to reply. If 30 April is a Sunday, the final date of reply would be Monday 1 May. If Monday 1 May is a public holiday, you must respond by Tuesday 2 May.

In some instances, firms have adopted a 28-day timeline to avoid any confusion arising from variations in the length of the month and public holidays.

Putting the Proper Processes in Place

Access requests can be time-consuming. The GDPR does not differentiate between large multinational firms and small businesses in this regard. All organisations are expected to adhere to the time limits.

It pays, therefore, to have a clear structure in place to deal with subject access requests (SARs). For example:

- Clarifying the identity verification procedures the business will use to confirm the individual is who they say they are
- Putting in place a SARs response team who will deal with requests in a timely manner. For large businesses, this will likely be led by the firm's compliance team. For SMEs, it may fall to the business owner and one or two senior managers
- Having clarity on response timelines

[27] 'Right of access', ICO, https://ico.org.uk/for-organisations/guide-to-data-protection/guide-to-the-general-data-protection-regulation-gdpr/individual-rights/right-of-access/

- Identifying who will keep a record of the access request, to demonstrate accountability under GDPR
- Ensuring that the business is clear on what constitutes a vexatious or repetitive request. Can this decision be backed up with facts?
- Having a consistent structure and format when responding to requests. For example, will the company list the main categories of data they hold, or provide more granular information?

Many businesses recognise the wisdom of good data management and retention policies only in hindsight. If you hold personal data on an individual at the time they make an access request, you must make every reasonable effort to supply it to them. It only takes a few access requests for businesses to realise that holding on to personal information 'just in case' it is needed, is a recipe for non-compliance and unnecessarily arduous data searches.

A business cannot edit, amend or erase data if they would not otherwise have done so, or in an attempt to prevent disclosure.

What Is a Proportionate Response?

Proportionality is a core principle of EU law; it applies to European directives and regulations, including GDPR. With regard to SARs, commentators and data controllers have debated what constitutes a 'proportionate' response. Law firm Fieldfisher, for example, notes that 'a balance must be struck between the ease with which individuals can submit access requests (for free) and the considerable effort, cost and third party privacy intrusions to which the controller must go in order to fulfil a single [subject access request].'[28]

Article 14(5) of GDPR states that the controller's obligation does not apply where doing so would 'prove impossible or involve disproportionate effort'.

For marketers, this means that there is still some uncertainty as to how best to comply with access requests. In many cases, firms have committed

---

[28] Richard Lawne, 'Subject access requests and the search for proportionality', Fieldfisher, 26 February 2020, https://www.fieldfisher.com/en/services/privacy-security-and-information/privacy-security-and-information-law-blog/subject-access-requests-and-the-search-for-proport

very substantial resources to trawling their databases for all references to the data subject. It is particularly difficult where the individual gives few specifics on the date, timeline or subject area they wish to focus upon.

How Much Information Should Be Supplied?

Another source of frustration for firms is lack of clarity on how much data to provide to the individual. Specifically, does the company need to forward a copy of every document mentioning the person (redacting third-party and other sensitive data as appropriate), or would a table or document setting out summaries of the personal data suffice?

A 2019 case in the High Court of England and Wales is instructive. In *Rudd v Bridle*, the court ruled that a summary approach is sufficient. It provided the individual with an understanding of the essence of the data being held by the company. Claimants did not have the right to 'know the full contents of the documents'. It further stated that 'information can be presented in intelligible form without the need to provide its full context, or even the whole of the sentence in which it appears.'[29]

Marketers should keep an eye on how best practice develops in this area. It is unclear whether a consensus will be achieved in the short term. For the moment, following closely the advice of one's relevant data protection authority and guidance from legal counsel is the most prudent approach.

The Right to Be Informed

Articles 13 and 14 of GDPR state that individuals must be provided with specific information at the time when their personal data is being obtained. This covers the following aspects:

1. The identity and contact details of the data controller, or their representative
2. The data protection officer's contact details
3. The lawful basis for processing, and the purposes for which the data will be used

---

[29] *Rudd v Bridle and another (Rev 1)* [2019] EWHC 893. See https://www.bailii.org/ew/cases/EWHC/QB/2019/893.html

4. If legitimate interest is being relied upon as the legal basis for processing, the controller must provide details as to the nature of the legitimate interest
5. Any other recipients of the personal data
6. If there are data transfers to a non-EU member state, details must be provided regarding safeguards and any adequacy decisions that are in place to ensure compliance with GDPR
7. The retention period for the data. Failing this, the criteria that will be used to decide how long the data will be kept
8. The existence of the rights of access, rectification, erasure, restriction, data portability and objection
9. If processing is based on the consumer's consent, the right to withdraw this consent, and that this can be done at any time
10. The right to lodge a complaint with the Data Protection Commission
11. The existence of any automated decision-making processes, including profiling
12. If required for statutory or contractual purposes, the potential outcomes from failing to provide the personal data

Under the GDPR's principle of transparency, this information must be provided in clear and straightforward language. There are additional requirements where the data has not been directly obtained from the data subject.[30]

As one of the main processors of data within an organisation, marketers must be cognisant of the above. One of the most common examples of the right to be informed, in practice, is the use of privacy notices on company websites. In the past, these have often been lengthy documents, filled with jargon and legalese. This is no longer sufficient. Under GDPR, marketers must ensure that the information provided is concise and in plain language.

If you have not already done so, it is useful to set aside time to review your organisation's privacy notice and other relevant data protection statements. Consider whether all the required information is included. Ask a colleague or peer from a non-marketing background to read the statement and see if they can interpret it correctly. If esoteric language

[30] For more information on these requirements, please refer to Article 14 of the GDPR.

or jargon is used, replace it with wording that is more easily understood. In some instances, it may be useful to layer the information. This allows consumers to look at a summary overview or delve deeper into the granular aspects of the data processing as required.

The Right to Restrict Processing

Consumers can ask organisations to constrain how their personal data is processed. Under Article 18 of GDPR, an individual can ask a company to cease processing for particular purposes.

This right applies in a number of instances. You can restrict processing that is unlawful, or where you require data for the purposes of a legal claim. The consumer can also object under Article 21, where direct marketing is taking place or where they are contesting the accuracy of the data.

In a marketing context, a simple example might be opting out of a newsletter mailing list. The organisation must comply with the data subject's wishes. Alternatively, a company might need to retain certain information, but the consumer wishes to make sure that it is not used for any purpose beyond those specifically defined, for instance if the data is needed to establish or defend a legal claim. Marketers should have clear procedures and structures in place to be able to manage such requests effectively.

The Right to Data Portability

The EU is keen for individuals to be able to obtain and reuse their personal data across different services. Consumers can thus move more easily between rival firms, getting the best value for money. Previously, many companies benefited from inertia on the part of customers who could not face the hassle of moving their bank account, insurer, utilities or other service provider.

The right to data portability is a new right under GDPR and it applies where automated processing has taken place and the data processed is on the legal basis of contract or consent. When responding to such a request, personal data should be provided in a structured, commonly used, machine-readable and interoperable format. Where technically feasible, the data subject should have the ability to have the relevant data transferred directly from one data controller to another. According to Recital

68, 'data controllers should be encouraged to develop interoperable formats that enable data portability.'

From a marketing perspective, this means that consumers can switch operators (for example their mobile company) more easily. Rather than significant form filling, their data can be transferred electronically to a new supplier.

There are brand implications for marketing teams, as consumers will expect to be able to move smoothly between firms. If your business wishes to maintain strong word of mouth and a positive customer experience, marketing needs to be involved in understanding and having an input into the process by which this is achieved. While primarily a compliance requirement under GDPR, its potential to impact on the company's brand is significant if it is done in an overly bureaucratic or haphazard manner.

The Right of Erasure

Also known as 'the right to be forgotten', Article 17 of GDPR gives individuals the right to request an organisation erase their data in certain circumstances, for example when the data is no longer necessary, no longer meets the legal basis for processing, or was processed in an unlawful manner. It also applies where the consumer withdraws his or her consent. It does not apply, however, where the person's data is being held due to a legal claim or other obligation under law.

Having a clearly understood retention policy, regularly updated, is paramount in order to deal with consumer requests to activate this right. It reduces the likelihood that data will be held for longer than necessary, identifies the relevant legal basis, and provides trust and transparency for consumers.

The right to be forgotten has received significant media attention in recent years, particularly regarding the perceived permanency of any information that is supplied online. GDPR takes account of this. Recital 66 states that in order to 'strengthen the right to be forgotten in the online environment, the right to erasure should also be extended in such a way that a controller who has made the personal data public should be obliged to inform the controllers which are processing such personal data to erase any links to, or copies or replications of those personal data'.

A particularly well known example is the Google Spain case. A Spanish national's house was repossessed in 1998 to recover social security debts.

He objected to the story being linked to him whenever his name was searched on Google. The European Court of Justice ruled that Google must delete 'inadequate, irrelevant or no longer relevant' data from its results when a member of the public requests it.

It is worth noting that there are a number of exemptions where this right does not apply. These include:

- When exercising one's right of freedom of expression
- If required to comply with a legal obligation
- For reasons of public interest regarding public health
- If the data is being used for archiving purposes in the public interest, scientific, statistical or research purposes
- If the data is needed in relation to a legal claim

Automated Decision-Making

Article 22 of GDPR gives consumers the right not to be subjected to decisions or profiling based solely on the outcome of automated processing, where the outcome has a legal impact.

Automated processing is permitted only with express consent, when necessary for the performance of a contract or when authorised by law. In these scenarios, suitable measures must be in place to safeguard a person's rights and freedoms. This may include the right to obtain human intervention on the controller's part, the right to challenge the decision or for the person to present their own point of view.

Marketers must be particularly cognisant of any profiling that utilises special category data, for example genetic or health data, or information relating to a person's ethnicity or political views. A higher bar is set in these instances. Express consent must be provided by the individual or there must be a substantial public interest rationale.

Right to Object

The right to object enables individuals to object to processing for specific purposes or in a specific manner, where it could cause significant damage or distress to the person. Data subjects have the right to object to direct marketing at any time. Where this takes place, the business must cease using that data for marketing communications purposes.

Other instances where individuals can object include:

- Where the data is retained for longer than necessary for the purposes it was originally collected
- Where the data has been unlawfully processed
- If the controller is under a legal obligation to delete the information
- If consent has been withdrawn and no other legitimate legal basis exists
- If the information was collected relating to 'information society services' (online services, such as social media) provided to a child

Recital 69 states that an individual can object where their personal data is being processed in the public interest, in the exercise of official authority or on the basis of legitimate interests. It is then up to the controller to demonstrate that its compelling legitimate interest overrides the interests, rights and freedoms of the data subject.

Why This Is Important for Marketers

Data subject rights are one of the main ways individuals can exercise protection over their data privacy. Marketers have a responsibility in how the company represents itself externally and are the voice of the consumer within the business. We must be seen to keep the needs of our customers uppermost in our minds.

Just as important is the requirement for marketing teams to respond in a timely manner to access requests, meeting the deadlines set by the GDPR. For example, if a member of your team receives a subject access request it is paramount that they are aware that the company has a maximum of one month in which to respond. A well-trained team, familiar with subject rights under the Regulation, will know who within the company they should follow up with to progress the request. They will immediately notify their line manager and the company's data protection officer.

In contrast, the worst-case scenario is that the request remains on the 'to do list', sitting among numerous other emails, only to be re-found with too little time to properly respond with the relevant documentation. As we have seen, consumers are increasingly conscious of their privacy. Companies that do not show due respect for individuals' rights risk financial penalties, and damaging their brand, their reputation and the trust they have built up with customers, clients and stakeholders.

7

Data Security, Data Breaches and Reporting

Chapter 7 at a glance

1. Data breaches are one of the most high-profile aspects of GDPR.
2. Ireland has one of the highest volumes of data breach reporting per capita.
3. Large fines have been applied to a number of global businesses. However, a consistent approach is yet to emerge across EU member states. In May 2020, Tusla became the first organisation in Ireland to be fined under GDPR.
4. Adhering to the core principles of GDPR and providing adequate security measures are important factors in how courts and national supervisory authorities decide upon fines.
5. When reporting a breach to the Data Protection Commission, controllers are required to self-certify the risk level involved. Companies need to give due consideration to assessing risk levels, to ensure that a consistent approach is applied.
6. It is important to have clear protocols in place as to how your firm identifies and responds to data breaches.

Data breaches have caught the attention of many consumers, marketers and the media. It is difficult to avoid, given the potential for eye-watering fines, which can be up to €20 million or 4 per cent of global turnover, whichever is the greater. In the UK, stiff penalties were proposed for firms such as British Airways (£183 million)[31] and Marriott International (£99 million).[32] In the case of Marriott, the fine was for a cyber-incident where approximately 339 million guest records globally were exposed. Seven million UK residents were affected.[33] In March 2020, meanwhile, Sweden issued a €7 million fine to Google for not complying with the GDPR's right to be forgotten.

According to a report by law firm DLA Piper, the Netherlands, Germany and the UK had the most data breach notifications in the period 25 May 2018 to end January 2020 across all European markets.[34] Total breaches numbered 40,647 (the Netherlands), 37,636 (Germany) and 22,181 (UK). When weighted for population size, the Netherlands, Ireland and Denmark held the top three places, with Ireland reporting 133 data breaches per 100,000 people. Given the profile of Ireland's Data Protection Commission (DPC), led by Helen Dixon, this is not surprising. The Irish media have covered GDPR and data protection issues in considerable detail in recent years.

Dixon and her team have faced criticism internationally for a perceived slowness in issuing fines, particularly in light of the number of large, data-intensive technology companies based in Ireland. This perception may change over the next twelve months. In May 2020, Tusla became the first organisation to be fined in Ireland under GDPR. It was penalised €75,000 for wrongful disclosures of children's personal data. In December 2020, the DPC issued Twitter with a fine of €450,000 for a GDPR breach at the technology firm.

---

31 'British Airways faces record £183m fine for data breach', BBC News, 8 July 2019, https://www.bbc.com/news/business-48905907

32 'Statement: Intention to fine Marriott International Inc. more than £99 million for data breach', ICO, 9 July 2019, https://ico.org.uk/about-the-ico/news-and-events/news-and-blogs/2019/07/statement-intention-to-fine-marriott-international-inc-more-than-99-million-under-gdpr-for-data-breach/

33 The proposed fines were subsequently reduced to £20 million for British Airways and £18.4 million for Marriott. The impact of the pandemic on the travel and hospitality sector was a factor in both decisions.

34 DLA Piper, 'GDPR Data Breach Survey', January 2020.

For marketers with a multinational remit, a consistent approach across EU member states has yet to emerge. The level of fines is still in flux, varying substantially from country to country. It will take time, possibly five to ten years, before a standard methodology emerges that will allow firms to accurately estimate potential fine levels and insure accordingly. One aspect that is emerging from initial fines is the focus placed on adherence to GDPR's core principles. These, and ensuring appropriate security measures for data processing, will remain a focus for supervisory authorities and the courts over the coming months and years.

Data Security

Data security is a fundamental component of the GDPR principle of integrity and confidentiality. Article 32 of GDPR provides a detailed outline of requirements. It states that 'appropriate technical and organisational measures' must be undertaken. This is to ensure that the level of security provided is in keeping with the type of processing activity taking place and the personal data held by the firm. It requires consideration of risk analysis, organisational policies, and physical and technical measures. Proportionality is key. Businesses must seek to balance the best available technological solution with the cost of implementing it and the potential risks involved in processing.

Inadequate data security can deeply impact a business. As described by Britain's supervisory authority, 'poor information security leaves your systems and services at risk and may cause real harm and distress to individuals – lives may even be endangered in some extreme cases.'[35]

Potential harm can include identity theft and targeting by cyber-criminals. These can have very significant consequences for those involved and affect the firm's reputation. Security measures must therefore be effective in a number of ways. Some examples are as follows:

- Appropriate access rights need to be in place to ensure that data cannot be altered, disclosed, deleted or otherwise accessed except by those with permission to do so. In a marketing context, careful consideration should be given to aspects such as appropriate user rights for

---

[35] ICO, 'Security'. https://ico.org.uk/for-organisations/guide-to-data-protection/guide-to-the-general-data-protection-regulation-gdpr/security/

marketing databases, newsletter mailing platforms, and customer relationship management systems. Procedures must be in place when staff move to another team or leave the company. In the former case, their user rights may need to be substantially amended; in the latter, access should be discontinued from the date of departure.

- Written processes should be in place to ensure that data is accurate and relevant. Relying on manual procedures leaves the company open to human error, duplicated and siloed data. These increase the risk of a data breach and reduce the company's ability to accurately audit the personal data it holds.
- Data must remain accessible and usable for the purposes originally intended. An inability to access certain data can cause significant distress, for example in the case of a medical or legal issue where the consumer needs to access their personal data urgently. Appropriate back-up mechanisms should therefore be in place.
- Regular training for relevant staff is also vital. Systems are only as secure as the people who use them. A team well trained in GDPR is far more likely to keep data security top of mind and act in accordance with best practice. For example, many firms still send Excel documents internally to colleagues without password protection. While this may seem harmless, it opens a myriad of risks, such as accidentally sending the file to the wrong person or recipients downloading and storing multiple, non-identical versions of the document across the organisation.

Article 32 of GDPR outlines a number of technical and organisational security measures businesses should consider:

1. Whether pseudonymisation,[36] anonymisation or encryption of personal data is required
2. The ability to ensure the ongoing confidentiality, integrity, availability and resilience of processing systems and services

[36] The Data Protection Commission describes pseudonymisation as 'replacing any identifying characteristics of data with a pseudonym, or, in other words, a value which does not allow the data subject to be directly identified'. For more information on pseudonymisation and anonymisation, see https://www.dataprotection.ie/en/dpc-guidance/anonymisation-pseudonymisation

3. The ability to restore availability and access to personal data in a timely manner in the event of a physical or technical incident
4. Instituting a process for regularly testing, assessing and evaluating the effectiveness of technical and organisational measures for ensuring the security of the processing

When undertaking a review, make sure to look at physical security and cyber-security arrangements. While cyber-security receives substantial media coverage, in reality there may be an equal risk from an unmanned or unlocked filing cabinet containing sensitive personal records.

Dealing with Third-Party Processors

Businesses, as data controllers, must ensure that they and the third-party processors they use are aware of data security requirements and comply with them. Contracts with data processors must be in writing, and include GDPR-compliant security measures. These contracts should contain information on the subject matter of the processing; the duration of processing; its nature and purpose; the type and category of data involved; the categories of data subject; and the controller's obligations and rights. In essence, the written contract obliges the processor to take all measures required under Article 32, and provide tangible proof to demonstrate compliance. We will cover this aspect in more detail in Chapter 11.

The Importance of Ongoing Training

Putting clear policies in place can aid clarity, structure and efficiency. They are also beneficial in demonstrating an active data protection culture in an organisation, and they help organisations meet the GDPR's requirement for accountability.

Another aspect for marketing teams to consider is the need for ongoing training. Many firms undertook GDPR training for their staff in advance of the introduction of GDPR on 25 May 2018. However, in sectors such as marketing, there is regular and continued churn as staff move onwards and upwards in their careers. For this reason, training must be an ongoing activity, for both new and experienced staff. Examples could include:

- A detailed module on data protection practice and policies as part of new team members' induction
- Half-yearly or annual training workshops for all team members who access or use consumer personal data in the course of their roles
- Clearly visible data protection policies and documentation that is reviewed on a regular basis
- In larger organisations, quarterly set meetings with the firm's data protection or compliance teams to maintain regular dialogue with this function
- Identifying a 'data champion' within the team, who will send the team regular updates on data protection and privacy trends, useful articles and other material of interest and relevance

Data protection is the responsibility of every member of your team. Implementing an active privacy culture helps keep this important issue top of mind and reduces the risk that lack of information, inexperience or forgetfulness might contribute to data breaches.

Data Breaches

Article 4(12) of the GDPR defines a personal data breach as 'a breach of security leading to the accidental or unlawful destruction, loss, alteration, unauthorised disclosure of, or access to, personal data transmitted, stored or otherwise processed'. In essence, a data breach means that the integrity, confidentiality or availability of the data has been affected in some way.[37]

One clear result of the GDPR's high profile is increased consumer awareness of their data protection rights. Since the Regulation was introduced, there has been a significant rise in the number of data breaches reported in Ireland. This is reflected in the DPC's 2019 annual report. A total of 7,215 complaints were received in 2019, a 75 per cent increase on 2018 figures. Data breach reporting, meanwhile, saw a 71 per cent increase for the same period.[38]

In a separate update, the DPC noted that 'of the breach notifications received in the first year since the 25th of May 2018, a total of 13% failed to

---

[37] Article 4(12) GDPR.

[38] DPC, 'Annual Report 1 January 2019 to 31 December 2019', https://www.dataprotection.ie/en/dpc-guidance/publications/annual-report/annual-report-1-january-2019-31

satisfy the requirement of notification to the DPC "without undue delay" (normally within 72 hours).'[39]

What to Do if a Data Breach Occurs

Marketers must undertake a number of actions in the event of a potential data breach:

1. Identify whether the incident meets the criteria for a data breach. For example, the incident must have an impact on personal data.
2. Once a breach has been identified, the firm must assess if there is a risk to the rights of the data subject. For example, if the data has been anonymised, no risk exists as the individuals cannot be identified.
3. If a risk does exist, the DPC must be notified without undue delay, and no later than 72 hours after the firm has become aware of the breach. If there is a delay, the firm must provide the DPC with reasons for this. As noted above, delayed reporting is still an issue for many businesses.
4. The company must make all reasonable efforts to secure the data.

Data breaches can take many forms, but are most likely to occur as a result of human error. Some marketing examples include:

- In response to a product or service enquiry, an email reply containing personal data is sent to an incorrect recipient.
- A marketer sending out a weekly newsletter includes the emails of a number of persons in the CC rather than BCC section of an email, thus exposing the contact details of everyone in the group.
- An incorrect workflow is designed on a customer relationship management (CRM) platform, resulting in personal data being shared with a large number of recipients.
- An attachment containing personal data meant for internal company use is accidentally emailed outside the firm.
- A former team member's user rights are not deactivated, giving her potential continued access to the firm's marketing databases.

---

[39] DPC, 'Information Note: Data breach trends from the first year of the GDPR', https://www.dataprotection.ie/sites/default/files/uploads/2019-10/Info%20Note_Data%20Breach%20Trends%202018-19_Oct19.pdf

Reporting a Breach to the Commission

The DPC requires companies to notify data breaches via a form on its website. This can be accessed at the following link: https://forms.dataprotection.ie/report-a-breach-of-personal-data.

The form is relatively user-friendly. It outlines the content to be included in the report. Criteria include:

- Whether the breach involves data subjects in more than one EU country
- If the breach is new, or an update on a previously reported incident
- A self-declared risk rating. The options available are low, medium, high and severe risk. Note: It is worth taking time, ideally with input from legal or compliance specialists, to identify a consistent approach to risk rating

In addition, the nature, cause and timeline of the breach must be described, along with the type(s) and category of data affected. Businesses must give a best estimate on the number of data subjects impacted by the breach, the likely consequences for them, and whether they have been informed. Lastly, the firm must identify what measures are being taken to mitigate the breach. These must be included along with contact details for the data protection person in the firm (typically, in larger firms this will be the DPO or head of compliance). A separate form is available in the case of telecom/ISP providers.

Notifying Data Subjects

In the event of a high risk to data subjects, the GDPR states that they must be informed of the breach. This must be done without undue delay, once the breach has been identified. Again, this requires the firm to make a balanced and proportionate risk assessment. Particularly notable instances might include:

- A scenario where special category or other particularly sensitive data has been exposed
- In the event of data relating to personal finances, where the data subject might then be exposed to fraud or monetary loss

In both these situations, it would be reasonable for the customers involved to expect to be notified immediately by the company. It is worth mentioning that some companies will notify individuals even where they ascertain that no significant risk exists. They do this in order to be as transparent and open as possible with their customers and clients. This can help build trust and accountability, and it is often the best approach. Too much organisational time can easily be spent mulling over whether a threshold has been met; far better, in the majority of cases, to notify individuals. Marketers will recognise the importance of trust for twenty-first-century brands. As the voice of the consumer within their organisation, I would argue that they should actively advocate such an open approach.

According to Article 34 of GDPR, the controller must include the following information when notifying data subjects:

1. A description in clear and plain language on the nature of the personal data breach
2. The name and contact details of the data protection officer or other contact point where more information can be obtained
3. A description of the likely consequences of the personal data breach
4. A description of the measures taken or proposed to be taken by the controller to address the personal data breach, including, where appropriate, measures to mitigate its possible adverse effects

Under GDPR, the supervisory authority has the right to compel the firm to make contact with the data subjects involved, if this has not already taken place and the authority believes that the breach poses a sufficiently high risk.

Keeping an Internal Record of All Data Breaches

Under GDPR, a record must be kept of all data breaches, even when it is judged that it is not necessary to notify the DPC or data subjects. In such instances, the firm should keep a record of the details pertaining to the breach. This includes the process for deciding that there was no risk, who reached this decision, and the risk rating attached to the breach.

The Importance of Clear Processes and Regular Data Audits

The above scenarios highlight the importance of regularly auditing personal data currently held and used by your marketing team. This ensures that you have clarity on what data is held, where it is located, and the retention periods involved. Failing to do so can result in ad hoc or ill-considered reactions on the part of the company. It is often difficult to keep a clear head in the midst of a crisis scenario such as a data breach. Investing sufficient 'thinking time' in advance significantly reduces this risk.

One of the best ways to do this is to identify a data breach committee or sub-group who will respond in the event of a marketing data breach. Depending on the size of the firm, and in addition to marketing representatives, this might include legal, compliance and other data protection specialists in the business. For SMEs, it may be a smaller group consisting of the marketing or sales director, the business owner and the head of IT.

Structuring Your Firm's Response to a Potential Breach

We have seen that companies have only 72 hours within which to respond to a data breach. Time is of the essence. It is important to note that the 72-hour window is not limited to the typical working week. If a team member identifies a possible incident on a Saturday evening, the clock starts ticking down from that point.

Therefore, it pays dividends for marketing teams to map the steps needed in the event of a suspected breach. These steps might include:

- Ensuring all frontline marketing staff immediately notify their line manager and the data protection owner in the business
- Convening an initial meeting of the data protection sub-group. As outlined above, this could be a small group in an SME or a larger committee in a multinational firm
- Identifying the initial likely scope of the incident; most important, whether a breach of personal data has in fact occurred
- Ascertaining what mitigating actions can be implemented immediately

Relevant members are tasked with further research and investigation. The committee should then meet again, as required, within the 72-hour period. Once all available information has been garnered, the data protection owner makes a final call on (a) whether a breach has definitely occurred, (b) if notification to the DPC is required and (c) whether data subjects need to be notified.

Waiting until your first data breach occurs is not the time to test these procedures. Instead, your firm should be in a position to react confidently, with a clear process and an understanding of the timelines involved.

Why This Is Important for Marketers

Data breaches are a key component of GDPR. Marketers, as one of the main data users in a business, are particularly vulnerable to breaches. We obtain data in a wide variety of ways, and communicate daily, if not hourly, with our customers and potential clients. This data is often stored on multiple platforms, depending on the activity involved. Such platforms can be located within the business, via its own proprietary systems, but also with a range of third-party service providers. Alongside this, marketing teams experience regular turnover as team members move to new roles or leave the business to explore other opportunities.

Having clear processes in place to ensure that data is secure can remove many potential risks of a breach. Regular team training and data audits are key, along with procedures such as clear access rights and a regular review of the user base across the company.

It is just as important to know exactly what to do when a data breach occurs. Businesses only have 72 hours to respond. This valuable time should not be spent working out how to react 'on the fly'. No matter what size the organisation, having clear procedures in place helps reduce the likelihood that mistakes will be made and deadlines missed. If your marketing team does not already have such processes in place, it is strongly recommended that you focus on this area as a priority action point over the coming weeks and months.

8

Different Data Protection Cultures

Chapter 8 at a glance

1. Different countries have different approaches to privacy, which reflect their own unique historical experiences. A notable example is the variation in data protection cultures in the EU and USA. This has an impact on each jurisdiction's data privacy laws.
2. Privacy Shield was one of the main frameworks for international data transfers from the EU to the USA. It was invalidated by the European Court of Justice in 2020.
3. Other options for Irish firms include standard contractual clauses and binding corporate rules. In future, this may also extend to approved codes of conduct, certification mechanisms and legally binding instruments.
4. The introduction of GDPR and recent data breach scandals have increased global consumer awareness around data privacy. They have also led to new local and state privacy legislation in the USA, most notably in California.
5. It is unclear whether a federal privacy law will be introduced in the USA.
6. Brexit has had a significant impact on data transfers between the UK and Ireland. Marketers must give consideration to what changes and mitigants are needed as a result of Britain leaving the EU.

One of the striking differences across countries and continents is in the approaches and values nations place on data protection and privacy. These have been forged over decades and centuries. In many ways, GDPR was a recognition on the part of the EU that local variances still existed across member states, reflecting their own historical experiences. These caused many headaches for businesses trying to operate successfully across the Union. Countries such as Germany and the Netherlands have dissimilar views, for example, on the use of personal data in business-to-business communications when compared to Ireland and the UK. In this chapter, we will cover some of the differences that marketers may experience and must be cognisant of in their use of personal data. This is relevant to marketing professionals working in multinational firms in particular, but also to the many marketers whose roles and career trajectories will take them to various countries and continents over the course of their working lives.

Many of the examples in this chapter focus on the different data protection cultures in the USA and Europe. We will consider how marketers can address these in a productive and respectful manner. The data protection implications of Brexit will also be explored.

It is worth noting that some of these differences are gradually being eroded. This erosion has picked up pace following the introduction of GDPR. However, of equal importance is the impact on consumer confidence arising from high-profile data breaches such as those that took place at British Airways and Marriott International. The combined effect of these has been to cause citizens of all countries to reconsider the value and use of personal data. Many people, both thought leaders and the general public, are beginning to question the inherent trade-off that exists as part of the 'surveillance' or 'attention' economies. These businesses are built on the provision of free services in return for obtaining and processing personal data. As more information emerges on how this data is used, trust is being eroded. Consumers are increasingly asking whether trading their data for access to apps, websites, online games and other digital products and services is necessarily a good thing.

Privacy Shield

One of the clearest examples of the different approaches to personal data can be seen in the EU–US Privacy Shield. This agreement, which had been renewed annually, was an effort by both jurisdictions to provide a stable and compliant environment for international data transfers between the EU and the USA. It was the subject of ongoing legal challenges by data protection advocates in Europe, most notably Austrian Max Schrems. The emergence of the Privacy Shield came as a direct result of the previous arrangement, known as Safe Harbor, which was ruled invalid by the European Court of Justice in 2015 following a challenge from Schrems.

In order to partake in the Privacy Shield, American companies signed up to the framework via the US Department of Commerce. Businesses had to live up to a set of data protection principles and have a privacy policy in line with these, with membership renewed annually.

Privacy Shield Declared Invalid

On 16 July 2020, the European Court of Justice declared Privacy Shield to be invalid, just as it had done with its predecessor.[40] The judgment took immediate effect and forced many businesses to undertake rapid recalibrations of their international data transfer processes.

The European Data Protection Board (EDPB) had raised concerns regarding the Privacy Shield. In January 2019, board members highlighted the 'indiscriminate collection and access of personal data for national security purposes',[41] a factor that led to the removal of Safe Harbor. The report also called for the appointment of a permanent US ombudsman and questioned that office's role in relation to US intelligence services.

Some of these aspects are mainly of interest to legislators and legal professionals. What is of concern to Irish and European marketers is the continued vulnerability of agreements such as the Privacy Shield as a compliance tool. Marketing teams that relied on the framework for transferring personal data to and from the USA had to quickly consider alternative and back-up options. Binding corporate rules (BCRs) were only feasible for large, multinational companies due to the significant set-up costs involved. Standard contractual clauses were thus the only viable

---

[40] DPC, 'DPC statement on CJEU decision', https://www.dataprotection.ie/en/news-media/press-releases/dpc-statement-cjeu-decision

[41] EDPB, 'EU–US Privacy Shield – Second Annual Joint Review', 22 January 2019, https://edpb.europa.eu/sites/edpb/files/files/file1/20190122edpb_2ndprivacyshield reviewreport_final_en.pdf

alternative for the vast majority of small and medium-sized businesses. We will look at these mechanisms in more detail later in the chapter.

State and Federal Privacy Laws

The introduction of GDPR and recent data breach scandals has sparked a renewed interest in data privacy in the United States, at both state and federal level. The most widely known of these, and potentially the state law of most relevance to Irish businesses, particularly those in the tech sector, is the California Consumer Privacy Act (2018) or CCPA.

The CCPA came into effect at the beginning of 2020. While not as comprehensive as GDPR, it mirrors many of its rights and principles.[42] For example, both sets of legislation carry broadly similar consumer rights to deletion/erasure (also known as the right to be forgotten), data portability and access. Irish marketers transferring personal data to firms or company offices in California must ensure that they are familiar and compliant with CCPA.

Other notable new state privacy laws include Nevada's Senate Bill 220 Online Privacy Law, which came into effect on 1 October 2019; and the Maine Act to Protect the Privacy of Online Consumer Information, which took effect on 1 July 2020. In New York, meanwhile, Governor Andrew Cuomo introduced the Stop Hacks and Improve Electronic Data Security Act on 25 July 2019. This law expanded the state's existing data breach legislation and cybersecurity obligations.

For marketers, compliance professionals and the firms they work for, this plethora of new legislation increases the level of complexity around data protection. Many businesses in the United States are pushing for a federal law that would supersede the current patchwork of state and local laws. Whether and when this will happen remains open to much conjecture.

International Data Transfers

Under GDPR, transfers of personal data outside the EU may only be carried out if they are in full compliance with the Regulation. Recital 101 of

---

[42] A useful comparison of CCPA and GDPR can be found in Laura Jehl and Alan Friel's 'CCPA and GDPR Comparison Chart', *Practical Law*, 2018, https://iapp.org/media/pdf/resource_center/CCPA_GDPR_Chart_PracticalLaw_2019.pdf

GDPR recognises the importance of such transfers for economic growth: 'Flows of personal data to and from countries outside the Union and international organisations are necessary for the expansion of international trade and international cooperation.'[43]

Irish businesses are increasingly taking a global outlook as they seek to grow and expand. There are a number of options available to marketers who need to undertake international transfers of personal data outside the EU.

The most commonly used is standard contractual clauses or SCCs. These are model data protection clauses approved by the EU. When included in a legally binding contract, they allow for the free flow of personal data. For most small and medium-sized businesses, the use of SCCs is the simplest and most effective way of dealing with international transfers. They can effectively be 'dropped in' to a contract, as long as they are not contradicted or overridden by other clauses within the document.

There are ongoing concerns regarding the continued viability of SCCs. An opinion from the EU's Advocate General in late 2019 suggested that companies considering SCCs needed to make an assessment regarding the equivalent data protection culture in the country where the supplier or data processor is based. Considerations might include the national security environment, local surveillance laws, and how privacy is respected in that jurisdiction. If the assessment is negative, contractual clauses may not be a reasonable mechanism to use.

The Schrems II decision in July 2020 also affected standard contractual clauses. The Court's decision cast doubt on whether SCCs provided sufficient guarantees for the safety of European citizens' personal data. As a result, in November of that year, the European Commission published a draft set of new SCCs, which it put forward for public consultation. Separate but related to this, the European Data Protection Board (EDPB) issued a proposed set of supplementary measures that businesses could undertake to ensure compliance with EU levels of data protection when making international transfers. Both documents generated considerable reaction amongst the business community. Many experts felt the supplementary measures, in particular, set too high a bar for companies and in effect created a barrier to international data transfers. Small and medium business owners argued that they did not have the resources to effectively

[43] GDPR, Recital 101.

assess 'if there is anything in the law or practice of the third country that may impinge on the appropriate safeguards of the transfer tools' being used.[44]

At time of publication, there remains a lack of clarity as to the final outcome of both the new SCCs and proposed supplementary measures. Their impact, however, will be considerable once approved. If your company could be affected, it is worth maintaining ongoing dialogue with relevant suppliers regarding alternative options that may need to be put in place.[45] Putting this in context, a recent report on corporate data transfers from the EU to the USA found that nearly 90 per cent of respondents relied on SCCs. European companies were even more dependent on this mechanism than their American counterparts.[46]

Another option is Binding Corporate Rules (BCRs). These are most suited to larger firms with a presence both inside and outside the European Union. BCRs are legally binding, enforceable internal rules and policies for data transfers within multinational companies. They are also expensive and resource intensive to put in place. Recital 110 of GDPR provides some further background, stating that BCRs are compliant as long as "*such corporate rules include all essential principles and enforceable rights to ensure appropriate safeguards for transfers or categories of transfers of personal data.*" Lastly, derogations also exist under GDPR. There are six possible derogations to consider, which align with the legal bases of the Regulation. These are:

- If the business has obtained explicit consent to carry out the transfer of a consumer's data
- If it is required for completion or performance of a contract

---

44 Experts have also decried the emphasis the EDPB placed on technical safeguards, compared to the other two pillars proposed – organisational measures and contractual safeguards.

45 See this useful review of the Advocate General's opinion and its potential impact on businesses: Marcus Evans, Lara White and Janine Regan, 'Schrems II judgement due in July – what this might mean for your outsourcing deal', Norton Rose Fulbright, 17 June 2020, https://www.dataprotectionreport.com/2020/06/schrems-ii-judgement-due-in-july-what-this-might-mean-for-your-outsourcing-deal/

46 'Advisor to the CJEU in the Schrems II case finds standard contractual clauses remain valid', William Fry, 20 December 2019, https://www.williamfry.com/newsandinsights/news-article/2019/12/20/advisor-to-the-cjeu-in-the-schrems-ii-case-finds-standard-contractual-clauses-remain-valid

- If it is in the public interest
- If a legal obligation exists
- If it is in the vital interest of the data subject
- If the firm can claim a legitimate business interest

These come with a caveat, however. The European Data Protection Board advises that derogations must be 'interpreted restrictively' and used mainly for activities that are 'occasional and non-repetitive'. As such, they do not represent a long-term, viable option for marketing teams or businesses undertaking international transfers of data.[47]

In future, there may be other mechanisms for data transfers. The GDPR lists approved codes of conduct, approved certification mechanisms and legally binding instruments between public bodies as three further routes to achieve compliance. These are all currently at a nascent stage in their development. For the moment, they are not an option for Irish marketers or businesses.

Brexit: An Issue for Many Irish Marketers

Brexit has put the issue of international data transfers back on the radar of many marketing teams. Now that Britain has withdrawn from the EU, it has the status of a 'third country', no different from nations such as Australia and Brazil. If your business uses UK suppliers for marketing activities such as customer relationship management (CRM) databases, HR or financial software, you need to revisit existing contracts and arrangements with these suppliers to ensure that they are compliant.

This issue can affect small and medium businesses (SMEs) as much as larger firms. SMEs located near the border with Northern Ireland, for example, may have multiple relationships with suppliers in the North, as part of a broader all-island economy.

At 11 p.m. on 31 December 2020, the Brexit transition period ended and the UK switched to its own version of the GDPR, known as UK GDPR. The Trade and Cooperation Agreement between the EU and Britain allowed for a four-month period during which transfers from the EU to

[47] A more detailed account of the EDPB's views on derogations can be found at https://edpb.europa.eu/sites/edpb/files/files/file1/edpb_guidelines_2_2018_derogations_en.pdf

the UK would not be considered as transfers to a third country. It can be extended for a further two months with the agreement of both parties.[48] The hope is that an adequacy decision will be achieved within that time frame. Under this process, the European Commission decides whether a country meets adequate levels of data protection. Such decisions are in place with a range of nations globally, one of the most recent being Japan.[49] Once achieved, personal data can flow from the EU to that third country without any further safeguards being required.

The UK has a strong data protection tradition. Its supervisory authority, the Information Commissioner's Office, is one of the most widely regarded within Europe and it is well funded. In spite of some concerns regarding the use of data by national security agencies, it is expected that Britain will be in a strong position to achieve adequacy. Data privacy experts had estimated the process could take up to eighteen months. However, it is likely this will now take less time, given the interim period outlined in the cooperation agreement.[50]

Marketers working with UK suppliers should take action now to ensure a smooth transition. For example, an Irish charity using a British-based database platform could take the following steps (please note this is for indicative purposes, and not intended to be exhaustive):

1. Audit what personal data is used on the platform.
2. Identify the types of personal data flows between its Irish office and the database platform.
3. Identify whether the servers used by the platform are based in Britain, the EU or elsewhere.

---

[48] DPC, 'Guidance on Transfers of Personal Data from Ireland to the UK at the end of the Transition Period (11pm on 31 December 2020)', https://www.dataprotection.ie/en/organisations/international-transfers/guidance-transfers-personal-data-ireland-uk-event-no-deal-brexit

[49] A list of countries with an adequacy decision can be found on the European Commission's website: 'Adequacy decisions', https://ec.europa.eu/info/law/law-topic/data-protection/international-dimension-data-protection/adequacy-decisions_en

[50] In a positive development, the European Commission in February 2021 issued a draft adequacy decision. It stated that the UK ensures an '*essentially equivalent level of protection to the one guaranteed under the GDPR*'. Remaining steps in the process include obtaining an opinion from the EDPB and getting approval from a committee composed of representatives of EU Member States.

4. Review its existing contract and ensure that SCCs are included in the document. If not, seek to redraft the contract and have it signed by both parties.
5. Update relevant privacy notices to continue to provide transparency to data subjects.
6. Document these changes to ensure the firm meets the GDPR's requirement for accountability.
7. Undertake a review to ascertain if any further actions are needed to maintain compliance with GDPR.

Why This Is Important for Marketers

Data protection laws are influenced by the history and culture of particular nations. This explains the different approaches to privacy legislation adopted by the EU and USA. Marketers must remain cognisant of these differences and plan their activities accordingly. Marketers are also required to be familiar with the legal bases for international data transfers under GDPR, as many firms, SMEs and individual departments use suppliers based outside the EU as part of their outsourcing strategies. Following Brexit, more marketing teams will be faced with this issue. It is important to put in place clear steps to maintain compliance.

Ongoing debates surrounding a replacement for Privacy Shield and the validity of SCCs mean that this is an area that marketing teams should monitor on a regular basis. It is prudent for senior marketing leaders to maintain ongoing discussions with their compliance and legal teams to assess the likelihood of significant upcoming changes.

9

Data Protection Impact Assessments (DPIAs)

Chapter 9 at a glance

1. Data protection impact assessments (DPIAs) are a key part of GDPR's requirement for data protection by design and default.
2. A DPIA helps a business to analyse and identify potential data protection issues relating to proposed new projects or initiatives that use personal data.
3. Undertaking this activity at the outset enables you to identify risks and put in place alternatives or mitigating actions to offset them.
4. The overall aim should be to minimise as much as possible any potential privacy risks and to determine whether the risk level is acceptable in the context of the project.
5. The GDPR allows for a flexible framework. DPIAs should be of a scale proportionate to the size, scope and potential impact of the project or plan.
6. There is no definitive template; however, many free templates are available which provide useful guidance.

Successful marketing teams are constantly looking at new ways to grow their business. This has always been the case. Advances in technology over the past two decades mean that there have never been more options available. As of April 2019, over 7,000 marketing technology platforms were available, according to Chiefmartec.com's annual survey.[51] The growth has been exponential. When the survey was first undertaken in 2011, there were only 150 such platforms on the market. There is a data protection implication for the majority of these services. From programmatic advertising to mobile applications and email marketing, most if not all of these platforms involve some element of personal data to deliver effective marketing solutions.

When introducing new processing activities, the GDPR requires businesses to implement data protection by design and default. 'By design' means ensuring that data privacy features, safeguards and technologies are considered and built into the project from its inception. 'By default' is linked with the principles of data minimisation and purpose limitation. It ensures that the service settings on a device or platform are automatically set to data protection best practice. Previously known as 'privacy by design', the GDPR now makes it a legal obligation to consider both aspects.

In reality, this means that projects with the potential to impact or process personal data should be assessed at the outset as to the risks involved. One of the best ways to achieve this is to conduct a data protection impact assessment (DPIA). Doing this ensures that the organisation meets its requirements for accountability, and can point to a transparent and documented set of procedures that have been used to assess compliance. This is the main topic we shall now explore.

A Mechanism to Identify Risks and Mitigating Actions

At its core, a DPIA is a mechanism by which organisations can identify potential risks and put in place mitigating actions to offset them. In some cases, where the risk is deemed too high, it may result in the project not proceeding or an alternative solution being explored by the business.

---

[51] Scott Brinker, 'Marketing technology landscape supergraphic (2019): Martech 5000 (actually 7,040)', 4 April 2019, https://chiefmartec.com/2019/04/marketing-technology-landscape-supergraphic-2019/

Marketers planning new initiatives that utilise personal data or combine it in new ways must therefore consider the data protection implications from the start. Too often, firms press ahead with an important project and retrospectively apply a privacy audit. Pressure from investors, senior management or competitors can be a strong incentive to push onwards. Under GDPR, this is no longer possible without first giving strong consideration to consumers' privacy rights.

In this chapter, we will look at how to implement a DPIA. First, we will consider the steps in assessing whether a DPIA is required. We will then look at the various aspects that must be factored into the process if a DPIA is deemed necessary. Even where not specifically required, DPIAs may still be undertaken. They show that the company is committed to best practice and transparency and they are useful as part of broader project management. Operationally, they can identify inefficiencies and eliminate unnecessary data collection or processing.

The GDPR does not provide a definitive DPIA template.[52] Article 35 offers guidance on the types of activity that would typically require such an assessment. This has been supported with additional guidelines from the EU's Article 29 Working Party (now the European Data Protection Board) and supervisory authorities such as the Data Protection Commission (DPC) in Ireland and the UK's Information Commissioner's Office (ICO). Many useful free templates are available to download, which can assist marketing teams seeking to implement their own DPIA.

If you are preparing your first assessment, seek feedback from your compliance team, legal counsel and others within or outside the organisation who may have previous experience of the process.

Is a Full DPIA Required?

The first step in any assessment is ascertaining whether a full DPIA is required. Under GDPR, a DPIA is mandatory for certain types of processing. These include:

52 Those seeking more detailed guidance can refer to the Article 29 Working Party, 'Guidelines on data protection impact assessment (DPIA)', European Commission, 13 October 2017, https://ec.europa.eu/newsroom/article29/item-detail.cfm?item_id=611236

- Where it is likely to result in a high risk to the rights and freedoms of individuals; particularly where a new technology is being introduced[53]
- Where it will result in automated decision-making or profiling
- Where systematic monitoring of employees' activities will take place
- In cases where sharing or transferring of personal data outside the EU will occur
- If it involves large-scale processing of special category data
- Where the organisation plans to implement systematic monitoring of a publicly accessible area on a large scale

'Large-scale processing' is not specifically defined. However, the DPC recommends considering the following factors:

- The number of data subjects likely to be affected
- The volume of data and/or the range of data being processed
- The duration or permanence of the processing
- Its geographical extent

To simplify the process, the table below includes a list of questions based on guidelines from the ICO and the Article 29 Working Party. This checklist allows marketing teams to make a preliminary assessment on the likelihood of a full DPIA being required.[54]

Question	Yes	No	Comments
Will there be systematic and extensive profiling with significant legal effects?			
Does the processing involve special category or criminal offence data on a large scale?			
Will the project involve systematic monitoring of a publicly accessible place on a large scale?			

[53] For guidelines, and determining whether processing is 'likely to result in a high risk' for the purposes of Regulation 2016/679, see Article 29 Working Party, 'Guidelines on data protection impact assessment (DPIA)', European Commission, 13 October 2017, https://ec.europa.eu/newsroom/article29/item-detail.cfm?item_id=611236

[54] Those seeking additional information and guidance should refer to the Article 29 Working Party's guidelines on DPIAs.

Question	Yes	No	Comments
Will it involve the use of new or innovative technology?			
Will profiling or special category data be used to decide on access to services?			
Will the project result in the profiling of individuals on a large scale?			
Will biometric or genetic data be processed?			
Will the project match or combine datasets from different sources?			
Will invisible processing (i.e. the collection of personal data from a source other than the individual, without providing them with a privacy notice) take place?			
Will the project track individuals' location or behaviour?			
Does the project involve profiling, targeted marketing or provision of online services to children?			
Will processing endanger the individual's physical health or safety in the event of a security breach?			
Will personal data be transferred across borders outside the European Union?[55]			

Typically, if you answer 'Yes' to two or more of the above questions, a full DPIA is recommended. We will now look at what is required to effectively complete that process.

How to Conduct a DPIA

Article 35 of GDPR advises that a DPIA should be carried out 'prior to processing'. It is best practice to carry out the assessment as early as possible. In some cases, a DPIA may need to be updated as the project develops.

[55] Recital 116 of GDPR notes the risks associated with such transfers.

It is the responsibility of the data controller to undertake the impact assessment. In some firms, the undertaking is outsourced to a third party; however, ultimate responsibility remains with the controller. Typically, the main driver is the project team; in our case, this would be the marketing director or manager and their team.

The more complex the case, the more important it is that a wide range of stakeholders are consulted. This will provide the breadth of views and experience necessary to ensure that as many risks as possible are identified. Different users and stakeholders will be affected in particular ways. Hearing a variety of voices ensures their concerns are listened to and, where proportionate and feasible, mitigated.

If your firm has a data protection officer, Article 35 of GDPR requires that their advice be sought. The data controller should also seek the views of data subjects or their representatives. Where this does not take place, the firm is required to document the justification for this.

Do I Need a DPIA for Processing Already in Place before GDPR?

The Article 29 Working Party strongly recommends carrying out impact assessments for all high-risk operations that commenced before the introduction of GDPR. A DPIA may also be required where a significant change occurs to the processing operation; where there is a change in the risk level associated with processing; or when the organisational or societal context has changed. As best practice, the Working Group recommends all DPIAs be reassessed after a three-year period.

The Steps Involved in a DPIA

Article 35(7) of the GDPR provides a broad outline of the minimum features of a DPIA. These include:

- A description of the planned processing and the purposes of the processing
- An assessment of its necessity and proportionality
- An assessment of the risks to the rights and freedoms of individuals
- The mitigating measures that will be taken to address these risks and demonstrate compliance with the Regulation.

Many firms have found this list somewhat vague and unsatisfactory when they sit down to begin an impact assessment. Data protection supervisory authorities such as the Commission Nationale Informatique et Libertés (CNIL) in France,[56] the ICO in the UK[57] and the DPC in Ireland provide advice, templates and guidelines to make the process more tangible. The following is a useful seven-step process for marketing teams to consider as part of their DPIAs:

1. Identify whether a DPIA is required.
2. Define the characteristics of the project and the proposed processing.
3. Consult with relevant stakeholders.
4. Identify data protection risks and the necessity and proportionality of processing.
5. Identify data protection solutions to reduce or eliminate these risks.
6. Sign off on the outcomes of the DPIA.
7. Integrate data protection solutions back into the project, if a decision is taken to proceed.

We will now look at each step in more detail.

Identify the Need for a Privacy Impact Assessment

In this step, you should broadly outline what the project aims to achieve. What is the business rationale for introducing the proposed project or platform? Based on the outcome of your completed preliminary assessment, you can summarise why there is a need for a full DPIA to take place.

Define the Characteristics of the Project and the Types of Processing Involved

Here, the project team outlines the type of processing that will take place if the project goes ahead. It is worth asking a series of questions to help determine the project's core characteristics and scale. For example:

---

[56] CNIL, 'Privacy impact assessment', https://www.cnil.fr/en/privacy-impact-assessment-pia

[57] ICO, 'Sample DPIA template', https://ico.org.uk/media/about-the-ico/consultations/2258461/dpia-template-v04-post-comms-review-20180308.pdf

- What data will be collected?
- How will it be collected?
- How will the data be stored and used?
- How long will it be retained?
- Will it be shared with any third parties?
- Are any elements likely to be particularly high-risk?
- Will it involve transfers within or outside the EU?
- Will any special category data be processed?
- Does it include personal data for minors or vulnerable groups in society?
- Is the technology new or relatively untested?

Many firms find using a data flow diagram instructive at this point in the process. Avoid the temptation for complexity. Any diagram should be simple enough to be understood by one of the firm's customers. Keeping this level of simplicity can be difficult for those with a specialist, technical or engineering background. It is worth remembering that the more complex the schematic, the less likely it is to meet the GDPR's requirement to be transparent and comprehensible. A useful rule of thumb is to ask a customer or other user to review the draft diagram. If they can understand the key points, it is likely that a layperson will be able to do so too.

Consult with Stakeholders

At this point, you should consult widely to identify the potential risks relating to the project. Different stakeholders and users may have particular examples or concerns your core team had not considered. Make sure to include the views of experts too. These could be IT, legal or compliance specialists, cyber-security consultants or those with software development expertise. Consider other important potential users, such as third-party suppliers, ethical specialists and data processors, all of whom may be able to add value.

Identify Risks and the Necessity and Proportionality of Processing

The work you have already undertaken as part of the preliminary DPIA assessment will be helpful here. It should instruct a focus towards particular aspects of the project that were flagged as high risk at the initial assessment stage. However, make sure to look at a wide range of potential risk factors; for example, in the event of a data breach:

- The potential for loss of control over how the personal data is used; this is a very current concern for products and services incorporating new artificial intelligence (AI) solutions
- The risks resulting from possible identify theft or fraud
- Whether the individual would suffer financial loss or reputational damage if a breach occurred
- Could it cause them physical harm?
- Would it impact on the legal rights of the data subjects?
- Are there are any other potential economic or social implications that might arise from the proposed data processing?

Take time also to assess the necessity and proportionality of the proposed processing. Is there a clear legal basis? Could the same outcome be achieved in a different manner? Is the proposed technology sufficiently well tested or understood? How will you communicate effectively to data subjects in a clear and transparent way how their personal information will be used?

Identify Mitigating Actions and Solutions

You should now have a list of potential risks. Categorise each as high, medium or low risk to the business. It is then time to identify potential solutions and actions that will mitigate or remove each of these. The consultation process undertaken with stakeholders will be helpful here. The ICO has a useful matrix on its website, reproduced below, which allows marketers to map the severity of impact and the likelihood of occurrence.[58] Proposed mitigants might include reducing the extent of processing, using an alternative technology, increasing training for key staff, or enhancing the cyber-security and IT infrastructure.

---

[58] ICO, 'How do we do a DPIA?', https://ico.org.uk/for-organisations/guide-to-data-protection/guide-to-the-general-data-protection-regulation-gdpr/data-protection-impact-assessments-dpias/how-do-we-do-a-dpia/#how2

Severity of impact				
	Serious harm	**Low risk**	**High risk**	**High risk**
	Some impact	**Low risk**	**Medium risk**	**High risk**
	Minimal impact	**Low risk**	**Low risk**	**Low risk**
		Remote	Reasonable possibility	More likely then not
		Likelihood of harm		

Sign Off on the DPIA

It is recommended that the DPIA is formally signed off by senior management, once the risks and mitigants have been identified. Many businesses will need this as a matter of course, with internal compliance procedures requiring that the board of directors, management board or senior leadership team review and approve the DPIA and its proposed outcomes. This is also a useful opportunity to review project alternatives in the event the DPIA advises that the proposed activity should not go ahead due to the level of risk involved. The DPC advises that the process should be fully documented, as part of the firm's commitment to accountability and transparency. Marketers should also note that where a high risk remains, even after mitigating actions, and the business wishes to proceed with the processing, the DPC must be consulted for advice.

Integrate Data Protection Solutions Back into the Project

As any manager will know, a plan without owners and key deliverables is unlikely to be delivered upon. The final step, therefore, is to ensure that there is a clear series of actions that integrate the data protection mitigants and solutions back into the project. This should be reviewed regularly to assess progress. It is worth assigning overall responsibility to a senior leader who has the authority to call stakeholders to account in the event of non-delivery. If substantial changes are made to the project brief, scope or scale of processing in subsequent months, the DPIA may need to be revisited.

Case Study

Jane is the marketing manager of a small Dublin-based tourism company. She and her team of two marketing executives are responsible for promoting archaeological tours, primarily to 35- to 55-year-old tourists from mainland Europe. Up to now, Jane has used spreadsheets and a basic database to track enquiries and potential customers. She wishes to introduce an online customer relationship management (CRM) platform to allow her to better manage this function. If she can set up automated workflows and reminders, it will allow her team to reach out to this audience in a more structured and professional manner.

Having prepared a brief and compiled a list of possible suppliers, Jane chooses what she thinks will be the strongest solution. Before proceeding any further, she decides to assess the data protection implications of the proposed platform.

She and her team consult the DPC's website to get a clearer understanding of how to undertake a DPIA. She also consults a friend in a non-competing firm who has recently overseen a similar exercise.

Jane and her team complete the preliminary checklist to see if a full DPIA is required. It is clear that the new CRM meets a number of risk criteria. Most notably, the platform will allow her company to merge and combine existing customer data sets to create much stronger profiles. The supplier's servers will be based in the UK, which creates additional concerns because Britain has left the EU and is now a third country under GDPR.

Working through a series of documented steps, Jane's team identify and outline why a DPIA is needed. They then describe the type, nature, scope, context and purposes of the processing that will take place using the new CRM, noting in particular any elements that could be high risk. As part of this process, she and her colleagues create a very simple diagram to show the various data flows that would take place. With this in place, they then consult with relevant stakeholders, including the company's data protection officer (DPO), IT manager and legal counsel. They also speak with one of the firm's main customers, to hear her views.

As a next step, they outline the necessity for the processing that will take place using the CRM and the legal basis they will rely upon. This step is particularly useful, as it allows Jane's team to identify whether any alternative options are available that could deliver the same results but with a smaller data footprint.

Having completed that exercise, they then document the likely risks of using the CRM, and identify the mitigating actions that can be undertaken to reduce or remove these.

At this stage, Jane consults once again with her firm's DPO to make sure that she and her team have not missed any important steps within the process. Finally, they seek the company's management board's approval and sign-off before proceeding. Jane agrees with her board that she will provide them with a progress update once a month.

While a number of risks were identified during the process, Jane is confident that the actions she has identified will sufficiently minimise and mitigate them. Jane proceeds to award a contract to the winning CRM supplier.

Why This Is Important for Marketers

Understanding when and how to use a DPIA is an important privacy skill for marketers. Recognising the need for data protection by design and default, a privacy assessment allows marketing teams to understand the nature and level of risks involved in any new project or initiative. Establishing an agreed template that is used company-wide can ensure that a consistent approach is taken across the organisation. It also allows managers and teams to learn from other departments and colleagues across the business.

Any training schedule for your marketing team, particularly those identified as data champions, should include a detailed overview of how to undertake both a preliminary assessment and a full DPIA. Senior marketers should also give strong consideration to completing an assessment for projects that are already active. Finally, remember to clearly and thoroughly document any assessments undertaken. This is crucial to meet the GDPR's requirement of transparency and accountability. It also provides a useful reference document, should the nature or scope of data processing start to diverge from its original purposes over time. This type of 'scope creep' can easily happen within organisations, particularly where institutional memory is at risk from a regular turnover of staff.

10

Data Retention

Chapter 10 at a glance

1. GDPR requires personal data to be held only for as long as necessary for the purposes originally intended. It does not outline specific retention periods. That is for each firm to decide, following careful assessment of the data held.
2. For marketers, a mindset shift is required in how we view the retention of data. More is not always better. It is no longer valid to obtain or retain data 'just in case' it could be useful in the future.
3. Having a clear data retention policy is one of the best ways marketers and their firms can maintain compliance with GDPR. The policy should be reviewed regularly to ensure that it remains relevant and up to date.
4. Make sure to consider hard copy as well as digital records when undertaking an audit or reviewing existing data records.
5. Regular audits can also be helpful in complying with the GDPR principle of data minimisation, highlighting where excessive or unnecessary data is being held.
6. Companies must be transparent about retention at the time of obtaining an individual's personal data. Privacy policies and statements should provide customers with clear, easily understandable information on retention periods. Remember to update these to reflect any changes to the data retention policy that may occur over time.

One of the key principles of GDPR is to not hold personal data any longer than is required for the specific purposes that it was first obtained. This is one of the more difficult concepts for marketers to align with. Traditionally, many marketing teams have taken the approach that more is better. For example, additional personal data might be sought on an application form or online survey 'just in case' it might be useful in the future. Similarly, email contact details provided for the purposes of attending an event may subsequently have been added to a promotional newsletter or mailing list for which specific consent was not received. Marketers are also regularly sold on the benefits of big data, machine learning and AI (artificial intelligence) as having potentially seismic impacts on business effectiveness; all these technologies are heavy users of data.

It is easy to see why this approach was adopted. Marketers are conscious of the limited time and attention span of their target audiences. Rather than having multiple instances of data capture, a once-off, large-scale request would reduce the need to return with additional requests at a later date. Key performance indicators (KPIs) are typically set in relation to the size of a marketing database (for example, increase by 10 per cent or add 1,000 new contacts) rather than the quality and relevance of the leads it contains. The recent focus on inbound marketing techniques has had some impact; however, old habits die hard.

GDPR changes this approach completely, and marketing teams need to adopt a new mindset. The benefit of the 'catch all' methodology is now substantially outweighed by the compliance penalties for firms that retain personal data for longer than lawfully required. In this chapter, we will look at data retention best practice. The first, and best, place to start is with a clear and comprehensive data retention policy.

Data Retention Policy

A data retention policy is the cornerstone of effective and compliant data protection practice. Alongside an audit of your company's data, having a clear retention policy and schedule is fundamental to knowing how long to hold on to particular data, the legal basis that underpins the retention period, and the rationale for having originally obtained the information.

Typically, all departments and business units in a firm will need to complete a retention schedule. The requirements will often depend on the business unit. For example, human resources and finance departments have specific legal obligations to retain records on employment and salaries for particular periods of time. Heavily regulated industries such as banking and finance may have similar stipulations from their regulator. The Central Bank of Ireland provides mandatory guidelines in the case of the Irish banking industry.

Most marketing teams will not rely on these types of legal or regulatory demands. Instead, they are likely to rest on the legal bases of contract, consent and the legitimate interests of the business.

Given the high turnover in marketing firms, particularly at junior and middle management levels, it is easy for the original rationale for data capture and retention to be lost with the passage of time. Key staff move on. Without adequate documentation, current data sets are retained unquestioningly – until a customer or client queries how their data was obtained and why they are being contacted. In the past, an apology and swift removal of relevant details from the database would suffice. In today's privacy-savvy environment, the likelihood is much stronger that the consumer will make a complaint to the Data Protection Commission, which may result in possible sanctions for the firm if not amicably resolved. Having a clear data retention policy in place avoids these scenarios.

Audit Your Data and Know Where it Is Stored

Before writing the policy, conduct an audit. Each department and business must understand the range of personal data they have stored, both hard and soft copy. Looking specifically at the marketing team, they must identify the types of personal data held. For example, does it include special category data or information relating to minors? How and where is it stored – in hard copy, on a server, in the cloud? Do we know why the data was obtained and is it still being used for those reasons?

Another issue relates to storage. Modern businesses are complex and use a variety of new and legacy technologies and systems. This has an impact on where and how data is stored. When auditing your marketing team's data, consider some of the following sources:

- Personal information hosted on your department's own servers
- Possible information held on third-party systems

- Information held by individual members of the team on their own laptop or desktop device; this is particularly relevant in current times, as people are increasingly required to work from home
- Information that is backed up or stored in archive format; for example, your IT team will often take regular back-ups of core CRM and database systems to ensure business continuity
- Paper-based file systems stored in the office or offsite

This process may take some time, but it is time well spent and will remove potential compliance issues that may otherwise occur at a later stage.

The Components of a Data Retention Policy

The baseline for any retention policy is that it is clear, transparent and written in language easily understood both by those within the firm and by customers and other stakeholders.[59]

In my experience, I have found that audits are useful beyond this core purpose, and can assist in complying with the GDPR principle of data minimisation. They often highlight cases where excessive or unnecessary data are being held, often as a result of the 'just in case' approach we mentioned earlier in the chapter.

Once the data sets are identified, the marketing team can allocate a start and end date for holding the information. Clarity is required in attributing the correct legal basis. For example, if a person consented to their email address being used to send them promotional information, this consent can be withdrawn at any time. Alternatively, if the information is being processed as part of a contract, for example when the individual signed up to the firm's service, the retention period may extend until the contract is completed and for a period of time beyond that. For marketers in particular industries, additional legal, regulatory or code of conduct obligations may also apply. It is useful to clarify these at the outset. The firm's legal counsel or compliance specialist may be able to provide helpful advice.

---

[59] The IAPP provides a useful data retention policy checklist on its website: https://iapp.org/resources/article/data-retention-policy-checklist/

The document should advise how any data will be destroyed upon completion of the retention period. A range of methods are available, including anonymising the data, permanently erasing it or, in the case of physical material, arranging for it to be securely shredded or disposed of. A specific individual or business unit must be identified as the owner who will oversee this task. Care should be taken that no risks arise during the disposal process.

In larger institutions, it can be easy for individual units to complete their portion of the task without anyone looking holistically at the overall procedure. For example, the housekeeping team collects printed files for shredding and leaves them at a designated location for pick-up by a designated supplier or third party that undertakes secure shredding. However, no one thinks to inform the site or office manager that the location needs to be locked or secured, potentially exposing the personal data to access by unauthorised individuals.

The policy must be flexible enough to allow for early deletion where necessary, for example where a customer exercises their 'right to be forgotten', or in the event the data is no longer used at an earlier stage than originally outlined in the schedule.

Once completed, the retention document should be approved by the company's management board and circulated to all staff and stakeholders. Where relevant, appropriate sections or an external-facing version should be made available on the company's website, providing transparency for customers.

Finally, the policy and related procedures should be regularly reviewed by the marketing team and the organisation as a whole to ensure that they remain relevant, accurate and up to date. This provides a timely opportunity to also assess what elements are working effectively, and which may need fine-tuning.

Access Requests

It is often only when an access request is made that a marketing team realises the downside of retaining large quantities of data. Once the request is received, the firm is obliged to respond within one month (or 90 days if an extension is necessary due to the size or complexity of the request) and to provide all personal data on the individual that is currently on file. This can be hugely time-consuming and a significant burden on resources. Retaining only relevant data and adhering to a clear retention policy minimises the likelihood that you will be found holding inaccurate, outdated or unnecessary personal information on your customers.

Multiple Platforms = Multiple Headaches

Like many sectors, marketers use an increasingly wide range of technologies and platforms as part of their daily work. This can make accurately tracking and auditing data a complex task. One of the most frequent issues relates to customers who wish to unsubscribe from mailing lists and promotional databases. For marketing teams, both SMEs with limited resources and multinational firms with a global footprint, this simple request can be very difficult to complete.

For example, a marketing team in a bank may have a legacy system dating back decades, on which the company stores core information about the customer. This is then supported by a customer relationship management (CRM) platform, hosted in the cloud, while promotional communications are undertaken via a separate system such as MailChimp or HubSpot. It is a sizeable task to ensure that these technologies communicate with each other. If an automated solution, such as an application programming interface (API), can be applied, the marketer can delete from one platform knowing this will be mirrored across the others. If this is not an option, time and resources must be spent on manually updating, increasing the potential for human error.

It is therefore timely for senior marketers to assess their current systems, not only from a marketing effectiveness perspective but also regarding ease of compliance with data protection legislation. We have seen that there are many, many technologies available to marketers. A data protection impact assessment (DPIA) should take account of the increased risk from adding additional data storage systems.

Exemptions for Archiving, Statistical or Research Purposes

Article 5 of GDPR allows for an exemption in the case of data used for archival, statistical, scientific or research purposes. This must be the only purpose for which the data is being utilised. Organisations and marketers cannot rely on this exemption as a way of accessing data sets outside these defined areas. Appropriate safeguards must be used to protect individuals' data used for such purposes.

Maintaining a Record of the Customer Relationship

There may be some instances where your team can delete a majority of the information on file. However, if the company needs to keep a record of its relationship with a particular individual, it may have to hold on to some data for an additional period of time, for example information on customers and enquirers who have asked to be unsubscribed from all future marketing and promotional communications. In this instance, the business has a legitimate interest in keeping a basic record to ensure that the wishes of the data subjects are followed.

Another example is where the business needs to keep track of access requests made by individuals. This is required to meet the accountability principle under GDPR. However, it can also be of benefit where the individual submits multiple requests over a short period of time and the business believes these are vexatious or unfounded. As with all aspects of GDPR, necessity and proportionality should be considered in each case.

Why This Is Important for Marketers

Having a clear understanding of the data that is retained within your marketing team is crucial for GDPR compliance. Failure to implement appropriate systems, procedures, documentation and training can leave you and your team floundering when faced with an access request from a customer or lead. It is important to know not only what data you have on file, but the reasons for which it was obtained and the legal basis for processing.

Data retention obligations also require marketers to consider what data they are capturing. In a GDPR environment, quality is far more important than quantity. The days of large databases containing old or cold leads should hopefully be a thing of the past, as compliance requirements come to the fore. There is an overlap in this message with the principles of inbound marketing, which argue for the importance of developing strong enquiry leads through a series of targeted steps.

Finally, as we will frequently see throughout this book, effective staff training is key. Human error is one of the primary factors in data breaches. Keeping data retention policies as 'living documents' within the organisation promotes a strong culture of compliance and best practice.

11

Controllers and Processors

Chapter 11 at a glance

1. In considering their data protection responsibilities under GDPR, marketers need to understand when they are a data controller or a data processor.
2. A controller has primary responsibility for how personal data is processed.
3. Controllers must ensure they have a written contract or data protection agreement in place with all suppliers that undertake processing on their behalf.
4. The processor can act only on the written instruction of the controller.
5. The processor must notify the controller at the earliest possible opportunity regarding any potential data breaches, issues of non-compliance or data subject requests.
6. In some instances, the concept of joint controller may apply.
7. The Data Protection Commission (DPC) has the power to take action against controllers and processors.

Marketers work with a wide range of platforms and suppliers, many of whom process data on their behalf. Examples might include a customer relationship management platform, a direct marketing firm, a social media or re-targeting agency. All these companies can provide increased targeting opportunities, to both existing and new datasets of current and potential customers. In order to do so, they typically need access to your team's databases.

For example, a social media consultant can use an existing set of customer profiles and seek to target a mirror version of these through Facebook, LinkedIn or Twitter; or a pay-per-click provider might request access to data from visitors to your website, in order to re-target these enquiries with specific messaging through a paid search campaign.

In each case, the consumer's data is being processed by someone other than your firm. To know your responsibilities under GDPR, it is important to be aware of what data controllers and data processors do. That is what we will seek to explain in the course of this chapter.

The GDPR outlines a range of requirements for processors and controllers, so you will come across quite a few lists of responsibilities. Bear with them; they will assist you and your team in achieving compliance and provide a 'ready reckoner' for any queries that may arise during day to day business activities.

Defining a Data Controller

Under Article 4(7) of GDPR, a data controller determines the purpose and means of processing. They decide why and how personal data is processed. A controller can range from an individual to a charity to a multinational company. The key factor is that they are in control of the personal data.

Controllers need to demonstrate compliance with the core principles of GDPR and with all aspects of the Regulation. They are also responsible for ensuring the compliance of any firms that process data on their behalf.

In some cases, two firms may be joint controllers; both companies exercise control over the data. In order to ensure transparency, Article 26 of GDPR requires that each controller is clear as to its obligations. This is usually achieved by way of a written agreement. This document outlines the duties of each controller, and how a data subject can exercise his or her rights under GDPR. For example, it might identify which of the two controllers would take the lead in responding to a data protection breach, notifying the DPC and acting as the primary point of contact for the supervisory authority. Failure to put an agreement in place can generate confusion, duplication of effort, and lack of clarity for staff and data subjects. It leaves open the real possibility of a data breach as each controller assumes the other is looking after certain aspects of the data.

Defining a Data Processor

A processor processes personal data on behalf of the controller. It does not own or control the data, and acts on the written instruction of the data controller. This contract is known as a data protection agreement (DPA). The controller remains responsible for how and for what purposes the data is used.

Under the GDPR, processors now have statutory obligations in their own right. They must maintain a record of all categories of processing carried out on behalf of the data controller. Data must be kept safe and secure. The processor must also assist the controller in complying with their requirements under the GDPR – for example, in the case of data subject access requests and breach notifications.

It is worth noting that employees of a firm are not processors. They are agents of the firm, acting to implement its requirements as a data controller.

Written Contracts with Processors: Putting DPAs in Place

Marketing is a fast-paced industry, with a focus on results. In the case of smaller businesses, such as SMEs, there may be relatively little red tape or bureaucracy required to offer a new supplier a contract. Marketers must be aware of the need to have a DPA in place with all suppliers that process data for their firm. This protects both the supplier and the marketer's business. The contract may contain model clauses, agreed by the EU, which specify that the processor will adhere to its responsibilities under the GDPR. It is also an opportunity to specify exactly what processing will take place, and who on the marketing team must provide authorisation in advance.

Under GDPR, the contract should include:

- The subject matter and duration of the processing
- The purpose of the processing
- The type of personal data and categories of data subjects
- The obligations and rights of the data controller

The contract should state that the processor shall:

- Process personal data only on written instruction from the controller
- Ensure that anyone processing the data commits to confidentiality
- Maintain the integrity of the data by undertaking all relevant and appropriate security measures
- Assist the data controller to fulfil its obligations regarding data subject rights
- Assist the controller in complying with data breach notifications and data protection impact assessments (DPIAs)
- Delete or return all personal data at the completion of the contract
- Provide the controller will all information required to help demonstrate compliance with the GDPR

Processors who outsource some of their work to sub-contractors will need to have written contracts in place with those firms too. This provides a chain of control that ensures the data controller is transparent on how its data is being processed. When outsourcing to sub-processors, the main processor must first notify the data controller and receive written approval.

Duties and Obligations of a Data Controller

If your firm is a data controller, it must keep in mind the following obligations in order to ensure GDPR compliance:

1. Maintain a log of all processing relating to personal data.
2. Display a privacy notice on all relevant communication channels, for example on the company's website.
3. Keep a record of data breaches and notify the DPC.
4. Ensure that contracts are in place between the company and its data processors.

5. Ensure the firm's staff understands the rights that individuals have under GDPR.
6. Carry out DPIAs where necessary.

In certain circumstances, the firm may also have the following additional obligations:

1. Designating a main establishment within the EU. This is required if the company has offices in a number of member states.
2. Appointing a nominated representative for the firm. This is necessary if the company does not have a physical presence within the EU.
3. Appointing a data protection officer (DPO).
4. Putting in place structures to enable the overseas transfer of personal data. For example, binding corporate rules (BCRs) or standard contractual clauses can be used when transferring personal data outside the EU.

A Checklist for Controllers

As the head of the marketing function in your organisation, it is useful to have a reference tool that the team can quickly refer to when ensuring ongoing data compliance. Atul Gawande, in his book *The Checklist Manifesto*, highlights the importance of checklists for today's busy professional workers.[60] Investing time in developing a checklist will help your team in their day-to-day use of personal data. Some examples are:

- Has your team carried out an audit of personal data used by the department?
- Does the audit identify and categorise this data (for example, identifying where sensitive or special category information is being processed)?
- Is the team clear about the difference between a data controller and a data processor?

---

[60] The book is a fascinating read on the importance of basic checklists. Modern professionals often work with structures so complex that no one person could understand them without teamwork and the assistance of other specialists.

- Are privacy notices in place on all communication channels where personal data is being obtained and processed? Are the notices regularly reviewed to ensure they remain up to date and relevant?
- Is a record of data-processing activities being kept and regularly updated?
- Is the team clear on its obligations regarding data subject rights and the lawful bases under which it can process data as a controller?
- Are contracts in place with all suppliers that process personal data on behalf of the team?
- Are procedures in place to identify and report data breaches?
- Is the team clear when to implement a DPIA and have they been trained on the documentation and processes involved?
- If data is being sent outside the EU, are standard contractual clauses (SCCs) or another appropriate mechanism in place to ensure that transfers are GDPR compliant?

Controllers and International Data Transfers

We covered the topic of data transfers in detail in Chapter 8. However, in the context of the duties of a data controller, it is worth monitoring closely. A majority of businesses use SCCs when transferring data internationally. These EU-approved model clauses can quickly and easily be included in a contract document with a data processor.

Marketers should be aware that the European Commission has proposed a new set of SCCs and is currently receiving feedback from industry and experts as to their applicability. In addition, the European Data Protection Board is proposing a series of supplementary measures that businesses must consider when transferring data to a third country outside the EU, where the data regime in that country does not meet GDPR standards. Firms should continue to monitor this area closely in 2021.

This is particularly important given the invalidation of the EU–US Privacy Shield, and with Britain now outside the EU. More businesses will be required to rely on SCCs. Again, keeping a watchful eye will ensure your company can take appropriate steps to put in place alternative transfer agreements with suppliers.

Sub-Processor Agreements

Some commentators have suggested that a set of standard clauses should be developed specifically for inclusion in any processor to sub-processor agreements. At present, there appear to be differing interpretations across EU countries as to the best way to ensure sub-processor compliance. For example, in the event that the main processor goes bankrupt or out of business, what rights does the data controller have with regard to the sub-processors this supplier was using on its behalf?

The Danish supervisory authority has developed a set of clauses to take account of this scenario. Under these, the processor has an obligation to provide its sub-processor agreements to the controller upon request. This allows the controller to confirm that they are held to the same data protection obligations. The Danes also included a clause whereby the controller can enforce the agreement with the sub-processor if the main processor goes bankrupt. It will be interesting to see if this is adopted by more countries, and whether over time it becomes a standard approach required under GDPR.

The European Commission appears to have taken this requirement on board. Its new proposed SCCs include a set of contractual clauses specifically covering transfers of personal data from an EU-processor to a non-EU sub-processor. Marketers should consult regularly with their legal and compliance teams to keep updated on the progress of these new SCCs.

Case Study

George is the marketing manager of a music store selling guitars and a range of Indian musical instruments. He has a database of 1,000 contacts who have enquired about his company's products in the past six months. George wants to re-target these potential customers with additional information and special offers relating to the products they viewed previously on the company's website. He has identified a digital agency, Optimal Targeting, who can re-target these customers through pay-per-click and social media campaigns.

Following a data protection impact assessment, George agrees terms with the business development manager at Optimal

Targeting. This includes a signed data protection agreement that advises exactly how the supplier can use George's contacts database.

The campaign proves successful. George is interested in exploring additional opportunities for growth. Optimal Targeting suggests an agency it works with regularly, which specialises in re-targeting through online banner ads. Having reviewed the proposal and undertaken a further privacy assessment, George agrees in writing to amend the DPA to allow for this additional activity, and for Optimal Targeting to work with the sub-processor. Optimal Targeting also ensures it has a written contract in place with the sub-processor.

It should be noted that in the above example, these campaigns are only lawful if a legal basis exists for the processing to take place, for example if the data subjects' consent has been received in advance. George will need to make sure the consent extends to this range of specific purposes. If not, he will have to re-seek it from his customers before activating the above campaigns. He must also update all privacy notices where the data is being obtained, so that he is transparent in how it will be used.

Why This Is Important for Marketers

It is crucial that marketers understand their obligations both as data controllers and, where relevant, as data processors. Each has specific requirements under the GDPR. A fundamental building block of good compliance is ensuring that written contracts are in place. If you or your team is currently undertaking a data audit, this is an important place to start. Any instances where suppliers are processing personal data without a written contract in place should be rectified soonest.

With ongoing changes to standard contractual clauses, alongside proposed supplementary measures, this is an area that marketing teams will need to monitor closely in the coming years.

12

Data Protection Officers

Chapter 12 at a glance

1. A data protection officer (DPO) is the person in the firm who provides guidance, assistance and advice to ensure compliance with data protection laws.
2. They are the company's main point of contact with the Data Protection Commission (DPC) and with consumers regarding data protection matters.
3. A DPO must be independent, have an expert understanding of data protection, and report to the highest level of the organisation.
4. Having a DPO helps demonstrate your company's commitment to accountability and best practice.
5. The DPO is not responsible for compliance; the firm as data controller remains ultimately accountable for any non-compliant processing.

The DPO is the main person responsible for all aspects of privacy and data protection in a business and an important compliance resource for marketers. Under GDPR, public bodies and organisations undertaking certain types of processing must appoint a DPO.

Articles 37 to 39 outline the designation, position and tasks associated with the role.

For marketers in larger firms, this will be a full-time resource or possibly even an entire unit or department. Many technology firms hire multiple data protection staff due to the data-intensive nature of their businesses. In smaller companies such as SMEs, the role will often be part-time, outsourced, or part of the broader duties of a senior member of staff.

Each firm must make a decision as to whether to appoint a DPO. This is based on criteria outlined in the GDPR, which we will look at in more detail below. Some companies that do not meet these requirements may still decide, on balance, to introduce the role to adhere to best practice. It is worth noting that the same duties and responsibilities apply whether the DPO has been installed voluntarily or due to a mandatory requirement.

Typically, the DPO will seek to guide and advise on data protection issues that arise during day-to-day business. They ensure that policies and procedures comply with data laws; provide input on data protection impact assessments (DPIAs); and act as the primary point of contact with the DPC.

When Must a DPO Be Appointed?

According to Article 37 of the GDPR, a company must appoint a data protection officer if it meets one or more of these criteria:

1. It is a public authority or body (except for a court acting in its judicial capacity)
2. The core activities of the firm require large-scale, regular and systematic monitoring of data subjects (for example, in a marketing context this could be online behavioural tracking)
3. Core activities include large-scale processing of special category data or data relating to criminal convictions and offences

While the first criterion is self-explanatory, there has been some confusion as to what constitutes 'large-scale processing or monitoring'. The Article 29 Working Party (now the European Data Protection Board) has advised that large-scale monitoring includes all forms of online and offline tracking and profiling.[61] This is particularly relevant for marketing businesses that offer behavioural advertising services, and for the firms that use these platforms.

The Working Party's guidelines on DPOs provide guidance on what could be considered large-scale processing. This includes factors such as the number of data subjects; the volume of personal data being processed; the range of data; the geographical scope of the activity; and the duration or permanence of the processing. If unsure, seek the advice of your legal counsel or compliance officer.

On balance, appointing a DPO provides a number of benefits. Most particularly, it shows that your company is committed to openness, transparency and best practice when it comes to personal data. At a time when many consumers distrust how businesses use their data, this should not be underestimated.

Tasks of a DPO

It is useful for marketers to be aware of the scope of a DPO's activity. The GDPR provides an outline of the types of tasks a DPO typically undertakes as part of their role. These include:

1. To advise a business on its obligations under the GDPR, as well as other EU or member state data protection requirements (for example, the ePrivacy Directive)
2. To monitor compliance with the GDPR and other data legislation. This includes the firm's policies and procedures, training of staff involved in data processing, the assignment of responsibilities, and compliance audits
3. To provide advice regarding DPIAs
4. To cooperate with the DPC and other relevant supervisory authorities
5. To act as the main contact point for the DPC on issues relating to data processing

---

61 Article 29 Working Party, 'Guidelines on data protection officers (DPOs)', European Commission, 30 October 2017, https://ec.europa.eu/newsroom/article29/item-detail.cfm?item_id=612048

Case Study

You are responsible for marketing a large online retailer with a presence in a number of EU countries. Cookie data on your website captures the purchase behaviour, search activity and geo-location of visitors and customers. This allows your team to create detailed profiles of each customer, providing them with bespoke offers and promotions targeted to their particular needs. The company is transparent about this activity, clearly highlighting it on its website and seeking opt-in consent from users. In this instance, your firm would require a DPO as this is profiling undertaken at a large scale (assuming the website has thousands or millions of visitors per annum) and across multiple jurisdictions.

The practical benefits for marketers are clear. With processing of this complexity, having a designated DPO to consult will assist the business in remaining compliant, accountable and transparent to its customers. In the event that the above processing was being proposed as part of a new project, a DPO is ideally placed to provide guidance to the project team on conducting a data protection impact assessment.

Training and Skills Required by a DPO

What skills and education should a person have when taking on the role of DPO? Lawyers and compliance experts have spent many hours trying to ascertain the exact training and qualifications a DPO should have in order to be considered 'expert'. Article 37(5) of the GDPR specifies that a DPO '*shall be designated on the basis of professional qualities and, in particular, expert knowledge of data protection law and practices and the ability to fulfil the tasks referred to in Article 39*'.

The Irish DPC provides some useful guidance on the expertise required, which includes: an understanding of processing operations; knowledge of IT and data security; knowledge of the business sector and organisation; expertise in relevant national and EU data laws, particularly the GDPR; and the ability to promote a data protection culture within an organisation.

It is quite a broad list. Most DPOs will be stronger in some areas than others, depending on their previous experience and route into the role. What is clear is that the scale of the business and its processing activity is a key factor. For example, a DPO for a small to medium-sized Irish business with no international presence would require less expertise than a global DPO heading up a team of compliance experts in a multinational financial firm. As the DPC advises, organisations must take into account the 'scale, complexity and sensitivity of their data processing operations'.[62]

For Irish marketers considering qualifications in this area, there are many routes available depending on the length and depth of study you wish to undertake. Two well-recognised options are provided by the Association of Compliance Officers in Ireland (ACOI) and the International Association of Privacy Professionals (IAPP). These courses lead to the Certified Data Protection Officer (CDPO) and Certified Information Privacy Professional (CIPP) qualifications respectively. On a personal level, I have found the CDPO training and designation extremely beneficial. This is not to discount the many other short courses and workshops provided by other suppliers. The DPC offers a helpful podcast series and a range of blog articles on its website that are very useful to those both new to and experienced in data protection. The most important aspect is a commitment to ongoing training and development in this area.

In 2020 the DPC launched a DPO network with the aim of sharing information and best practice with data protection officers throughout the country. This can only be of benefit as DPOs in diverse sectors share their experiences, questions and concerns with peers and can seek guidance from the commissioner and her team.

The Position of DPO

The GDPR also gives some detail on the position of the DPO within a business. Article 38 provides six aspects to ensure that the DPO can perform their role effectively:

1. The business must ensure that the DPO is involved fully and in a timely manner in all issues relating to the protection of personal data.
2. The DPO must receive support from the business; in other words, the firm should provide adequate resources for the DPO to carry out

[62] DPC, 'Guidance on appropriate qualifications for a Data Protection Officer (DPO)', https://www.dataprotection.ie/en/organisations/know-your-obligations/data-protection-officrs/guidance-appropriate-qualifications

their tasks, and access to personal data and processing operations to maintain their expert knowledge.

3. The DPO will report to the highest management level. Typically, this is a management board, CEO or board of directors. The DPO must be independent, and should not be dismissed or penalised for performing his or her tasks.
4. Individuals can contact the DPO regarding all issues relating to their personal data and their rights under GDPR.
5. The DPO is bound by secrecy or confidentiality concerning the performance of their tasks.
6. The DPO may fulfil other tasks and duties, but these should not result in a conflict of interest.

The last point is of significant relevance to marketers. While it is possible for a DPO to hold the position as part of a broader role within the business, those other responsibilities should not create a conflict of interest. For best practical reasons, large-scale data users within the business – for example the marketing director, head of IT or head of human resources – should ideally not hold the DPO role. There is considerable potential for their interests to clash with those of the DPO in relation to how data is used and processed in the organisation.

For example, a head of marketing under pressure to meet end-of-quarter targets may have the opportunity to drive additional sales through improved profiling of customers by combining existing data sets. If he or she also holds the DPO role, it would be difficult to be impartial when marketing benefits clearly accrue from the processing. At a minimum, the optics are not ideal. In some firms, having a number of data protection 'leads' or a data protection committee may be beneficial. Here, the conflicted person 'steps out of the room' when a potential conflict of interest arises.

Marketers and the DPO

As processors of a lot of personal data, it is likely that marketers will be in regular contact with the DPO and his or her team. It is useful to establish a strong connection. Provide the DPO with a clear understanding of the types of processing and activities the marketing team undertakes. Having a detailed knowledge of the types of data held, adherence to retention schedules, and the legitimate bases for processing will give your firm's DPO confidence that marketing places a high priority on data protection compliance.

There is a shared interest for both parties. Senior marketers know the damage a serious data breach can cause to the firm's brand and reputation, something that is not easily recovered. The DPO, meanwhile, will want a strong relationship in order to properly audit the business's data flows and processing as well as swiftly expediting data subjects' rights, for example subject access requests.

Why This Is Important for Marketers

DPOs face a complex environment. Rapidly changing technologies pose new and unique compliance challenges. Added to this, the increasingly fragmented global privacy landscape means that DPOs with an international remit must constantly monitor changes in relevant local and national laws in the countries within which their firm operates. The GDPR promised a harmonised environment across EU member states, but this is still an aspiration, and many local variations still exist.

Taking this into account, the DPO is an important figure with whom marketers should develop a good working relationship. Their knowledge of compliance best practice and mechanisms such as SCCs and DPIAs are invaluable. Building a strong, trusted relationship with the DPO in your company can help the marketing team avoid potential compliance pitfalls and assist in developing a strong and respectful privacy culture across the organisation.

Marketers should also not be fearful of strengthening their own knowledge in this area, whether by attaining a professional designation, attending workshops and seminars, or simply committing fully to ongoing GDPR training. This will serve one's career, customers and company equally well. Data is and will remain a fundamental building block of the twenty-first-century economy.

13

Direct Marketing

Chapter 13 at a glance

1. The GDPR recognises marketing as a legitimate business activity.
2. Marketers typically require consent before they can market directly to consumers.
3. There are different compliance standards depending on how invasive of a person's privacy the communication is perceived to be. For example, an opt-out option is sufficient for postal and telemarketing, whereas text messages and mobile calls must have the consumer's prior consent.
4. For business customers, an opt-out option can be provided. The details must have been sourced in the course of normal commercial activity or from a register of business contacts.
5. There is some difference of interpretation between mainland Europe (particularly Germany and the Netherlands) and the UK and Ireland with regard to business-to-business (B2B) marketing.
6. The GDPR and Irish Data Protection Act 2018 forbid direct marketing and micro-targeting to children.

Direct marketing is a core function of all marketing teams. From electronic communications to postal and telemarketing, it is a way to speak directly to individual contacts and customers. Each year, a significant number of complaints are made to the Data Protection Commission (DPC) relating to this activity. Consumers appear to find it particularly off-putting and invasive. The DPC's 2019 annual report states that 165 new complaints were investigated that year in respect of various forms of electronic direct marketing.

The GDPR and Irish Data Protection Act 2018 both contain specific references to the use of personal data for marketing purposes. Recital 47 of the GDPR recognises marketing as a legitimate business activity. In this chapter, we will consider what marketers need to keep top of mind when undertaking offline and electronic direct marketing.

What Is Direct Marketing?

A useful place to start is with a definition of direct marketing. At a time in our profession when long-established techniques are being renamed or rebadged, let's take a minute to clarify what we mean by this term. The best place to begin is with the DPC's definition:[63]

> ***Direct marketing involves a person being targeted as an individual, and the marketer attempting to promote a product or service, or attempting to get the person to request additional information about a product or service.***

The DPC goes on to identify what is outside the scope of direct marketing:

> ***Unaddressed mail received at your home is not covered by data protection legislation as no personal data is used. It also does not include market surveys seeking your views on say political matters or radio listenership preferences.***

The General Rule

As a general rule, direct marketing requires the affirmative consent of the person receiving the communication. This consent can be withdrawn at

[63] DPC, 'Rules for electronic and direct marketing', https://www.dataprotection.ie/en/organisations/rules-electronic-and-direct-marketing

any time, and is covered under Regulation 13 of the Irish ePrivacy Regulations (SI 336/2011). In addition, Article 21 of the GDPR gives the individual the right to object to the use of their personal data for marketing purposes.

Having established this overarching approach, we will now consider how it applies in the case of businesses marketing to customers, non-customers, to minors, and in a business-to-business setting.

Marketing Directly to the Consumer

Businesses typically require the consent of an individual before they can use personal data for marketing purposes. In order to provide transparency, when obtaining personal data marketers must clearly outline how it will be used.

Each time the consumer is marketed to, the business must identify itself and provide the opportunity for the person to withdraw consent. With online and offline direct marketing, this is typically done by way of an unsubscribe option. It should be as easy for the customer to withdraw consent as it was for them to provide it in the first place. This practice is not as common as it should be. Many of us experience the frustration of searching for a miniscule or hard to find unsubscribe button, then having to take multiple steps to withdraw our consent. At that point, we may still be met with nudge communications asking if we are sure about our decision. Apart from GDPR, this is a poor user experience; one that consumers will be less and less likely to tolerate.

Different forms of direct marketing require different types of consent. Core to this is the principle of proximity: how invasive is the communication to the person's life? For example, a direct mail letter by post will have a lower threshold of consent than a text message sent to the person's phone. The latter is deemed more intrusive.

Opting In and Opting Out

Marketers must be cognisant of this variance in compliance requirements depending on the type of direct marketing that takes place. As discussed, this is largely guided by how invasive the particular marketing channel is perceived to be. A list of some of the key channels is included below.

- Postal marketing:
  * Businesses can send direct marketing to non-customers using the names and addresses on the edited electoral register; this list includes all households who have not expressed a wish to opt out of such communications.
  * A company can post direct marketing to its customers as long as they are told in advance that their information will be used for this purpose, and they are offered the choice to opt out at that time.
  * In each of the above cases, customers and non-customers must have the option in each mailing to unsubscribe from any future communication.
- Mobile phone marketing:
  * Mobile calls and text messages require prior consent.
  * An unsubscribe option must be included with each communication.
- Telemarketing or phone marketing:
  * Firms can contact customers, but must inform them in advance of their intention to do so, and provide the option to opt out at that time.
  * In the case of individuals who are not customers, marketers must check the National Directory Database to see whether these persons have opted out from receiving marketing calls.
- Email marketing:
  * Customers must be informed at the point of sale, and given the option to opt out.
  * For those who don't opt out, businesses are allowed to contact their existing customers within twelve months of the sale, as long as the product or service is similar to what was purchased.
  * An opt-out or unsubscribe option must be provided with each email.
  * Communications can continue to be sent, presuming the customer does not withdraw their consent, as long as they are sent within twelve months of the previous correspondence.
  * Firms have 28 days to act on an unsubscribe request.
  * In the case of non-customers, prior consent is always required. This must meet the GDPR requirement of being a clear, affirmative action on the part of the individual; for example, ticking a consent box.

Where a business wishes to obtain a customer's consent using a tick box, this must be clearly and prominently displayed and stand out as separate from the terms and conditions of the sale.

Business-to-Business Marketing

There is a lack of consensus across the EU regarding business-to-business or B2B marketing. In some countries, such as the Netherlands and Germany, consent is typically required before a firm can promote its products or services to a business customer, but Ireland takes a more relaxed approach. Typically, Irish (and UK) firms rely on a legitimate interest basis when sending communications to business customers. Direct marketing is considered compliant as long as the data has been collected in the course of normal commercial activity or has been sourced from a register of business contacts. However, Irish firms must adhere to the wishes of a B2B customer that withdraws its consent. This must be actioned within the standard 28-day response time.

As the GDPR becomes more established and case law develops, it will be interesting to see what changes might occur in B2B communications. The proposed ePrivacy Regulation (ePR), which seeks to ensure the confidentiality of electronic communications, may have a significant role. Drafts of the Regulation suggest that B2B communication may move closer to the German model if ePR is adopted.

Workshops, Conferences and Events

We will take a short detour at this point to consider data used for the purposes of workshops, conferences and events, as it is an important part of business-to-business marketing. The DPC released a blog article on its website to allay concerns regarding the use of attendee lists and name tags at conferences. It's a great example of how a little information can be a dangerous thing, when it comes to how the public has interpreted aspects of GDPR. Among the sage advice provided, the piece states:

> *While it might be good manners and good practice to ask someone's permission to share their details through name badges or an attendance list, it's not true that this can only be done on the basis of the participant's consent. In these situations, organisers may want*

to consider whether another legal basis is more appropriate to rely on other than consent.

The article is well worth reading for those involved in business conferences and workshops. It highlights how other lawful bases such as legitimate business interest can be considered in such circumstances.[64]

Marketing to Children

The Data Protection Act[65] forbids direct marketing to and micro-targeting of children. Under the DPA, a minor is any child under sixteen years old. The GDPR requires that marketers be aware of the audience they are targeting. This is of particular relevance for businesses promoting goods or services aimed at children. Recital 38 of the GDPR states that children are less aware of risks, and any communication to them must take this into account. For example, language that might be transparent to an adult may not be easily understood by a minor. A higher bar of compliance is therefore required. A useful way to test the transparency of privacy notices and data policies for a young audience is to consult with this group directly, with the consent of their parents or guardians. If they cannot clearly understand the message, it needs to be edited until clarity is achieved.

In some cases, it may be beneficial to get the consent of both the parent/guardian and the child. Take, for example, a summer camp run by a local school and aimed at fifteen-year-olds. While they are under the legal threshold of sixteen years of age, they would still have a reasonable expectation that their views would be considered and may balk at the idea that their parents would make the decision without consulting them. As with all aspects of GDPR, marketers must consider what is reasonable and proportionate in such cases.

Penalties

Substantial fines can be levied on businesses that breach data protection rules with their direct marketing. They can amount to up to €5,000 per

---

[64] DPC, 'Does the GDPR really say that? – Attendee lists and name tage', 28 February 2020, https://www.dataprotection.ie/en/dpc-guidance/blogs/does-gdpr-really-say-attendee-lists-and-name-tags

[65] Section 30, Data Protection Act 2018.

instance of a breach, a figure that can quickly aggregate to a very substantial sum of money if the breach relates to a large number of contacts. Of 165 complaints investigated by the DPC under the ePrivacy Regulations, prosecutions were concluded against four entities, for a total of nine offences. Further information on current direct marketing best practice can be found on the DPC's website.[66]

Case Study

Oisín oversees the marketing of a small tourism adventure and recreation centre based in Mayo. He wishes to promote a recently built rope-walk activity to develop a new revenue stream for the company. He decides to use direct marketing as his main promotion channel. Available to him is a list of 500 customers who have used the centre's services in the past five years.

Oisín first filters the database by those who have used the service in the past twelve months. He then applies an extra filter to ensure that the service used by these individuals is sufficiently similar to the rope-walk activity he is seeking to promote. He excludes, for example, those who have only used spa facilities at the centre. He also checks his records to make sure that none of these customers opted out of receiving future marketing communications.

Oisín now has a filtered database of 250 contacts to whom he can legitimately promote the new rope-walk. He decides to use an email marketing tool. This has the benefit of a built-in unsubscribe function and can be electronically linked with the firm's marketing database through the use of an API. It removes the need to manually update any unsubscribers in response to the mailing, a risk factor identified when he undertook a DPIA. Having undertaken a final review with the firm's data protection officer, Oisín circulates the email to his customer database.

---

[66] For the DPC's latest guidelines, see 'Rules for electronic and direct marketing', https://www.dataprotection.ie/en/organisationsrules-electronic-and-direct-marketing

Why This Is Important for Marketers

We have seen that direct marketing is a core activity for marketing professionals. It is an area that requires a solid understanding of the types of consent required, depending on the activity being undertaken. This can cause uncertainty if not fully grasped.

Another aspect that causes confusion is the interconnection of the GDPR and ePrivacy Regulations when it comes to e-direct marketing. This is primarily covered via the latter Regulation, which is specifically intended to safeguard the privacy of electronic communications. However, there is an overlap, as consent, for example, must meet the threshold set out under GDPR – freely given, unambiguous, specific and informed.

Marketers are also using multiple platforms for electronic promotions. This increases the challenge of managing opt-ins and unsubscribes. In certain cases, legacy systems are unable to link with current marketing technology, leading to a requirement for manual updates and a significantly bigger risk of non-compliance due to human error.

Marketers should also be aware of the different thresholds that exist when direct marketing to consumers, minors and for business-to-business purposes.

This is a changing environment, with plans still ongoing to overhaul the ePrivacy Directive that underpins the Irish legislation regarding electronic communications. Marketers need to keep a close eye on developments in this area. It is worthwhile requesting regular updates from your data protection officer or compliance team. If a data champion has been identified within the department, ensure that he or she checks regularly for progress updates on the legislation.

14

Data Protection Training and Development for Your Team

Chapter 14 at a glance

1. Most data protection breaches are due to human error.
2. Induction and regular training for marketing teams is an essential part of data protection best practice.
3. Data protection is an ongoing requirement. It needs a continual commitment to upskilling and reskilling one's team.
4. Having an identified 'champion' within a department or business unit is a great way to keep data privacy at the forefront of your team's minds.
5. GDPR compliance is the responsibility of all members of staff. Claiming ignorance or an unwillingness to engage are not effective strategies.
6. As technological competency increasingly defines modern marketing professionals, a deep understanding of data privacy principles will be extremely advantageous for the next generation of marketers.

Most data breaches result from human error. It is a major source of risk for businesses and their marketing teams. Studies undertaken in the UK have found that human error accounts for up to 90 per cent of all breaches.[67] The International Association of Privacy Professionals (IAPP) advises that 'seasoned privacy professionals ... know that in reality the majority of incidents are inadvertent and unintentional.'[68]

It pays, therefore, to spend time implementing a clear training and development programme to keep new and current staff up to speed on data protection principles and best practice.

Human error covers a wide range of mistakes. It can be as simple as an employee clicking the CC rather than BCC option when sending a group email. However, there are many other ways breaches can occur, from unauthorised access and excessive user privileges to poor password protection, using email as a filing system, and sharing passwords with others. In a busy marketing department, it can be easy to let such practices pass unremarked in the effort to deliver quarterly or annual targets.

Breaches can result from inaction too. In 2018, a German data protection authority fined a social media firm €20,000 as a result of a data breach where hackers stole 330,000 passwords and email addresses. Upon investigation, it was found that the firm had stored the addresses in plain text format, a clear breach of its data security requirements under GDPR.[69]

In this chapter, we will look at the components of a robust training approach for your marketing team. Investing time upfront will protect your business from significant financial and reputational impacts caused by non-compliance with GDPR.

---

67 Anthony Spadafora, '90 percent of data breaches are caused by human error', *TechRadar*, 8 May 2018, https://www.techradar.com/news/90-percent-of-data-breaches-are-caused-by-human-error

68 Mahmood Sher-Jan, 'Data indicates human error prevailing cause of breaches, incidents', IAPP, 26 June 2018, https://iapp.org/news/a/data-indicates-human-error-prevailing-cause-of-breaches-incidents/

69 'LfDI Baden-Württemberg verhängt sein erstes Bußgeld in Deutschland nach der DS-GVO' ('LfDi Baden-Württemberg imposes its first fine in Germany under the GDPR'), Baden-Württemberg State Commissioner for Data Protection and Freedom of Information', 22 November 2019, https://www.baden-wuerttemberg.datenschutz.de/lfdi-baden-wuerttemberg-verhaengt-sein-erstes-bussgeld-in-deutschland-nach-der-ds-gvo/

Reducing Human Error

The author Carlos Perez advises that 'natural stupidity is more dangerous than artificial intelligence'.[70] It's a pointed way to make his argument at a time when popular media is focused on the potential pitfalls of machine learning. However, there is little doubt that reducing human error must be a focus of any data protection training and development plan.

Training programmes must be considered for new inductees and current staff. Induction is a great opportunity to highlight the importance the firm places on data privacy and ensure that new recruits are aware of core elements of GDPR such as the legal bases for processing, the seven principles of data protection, and individuals' rights.

However, it is a commitment to continuous training, upskilling and reskilling that sets apart those businesses truly committed to achieving an effective data privacy culture.

Senior marketing leaders should meet regularly with their human resources and compliance colleagues and seek to put in place a schedule of workshops and training sessions on GDPR requirements. These can take a variety of formats:

1. Lunchtime presentations from legal, compliance or data privacy experts
2. Encouraging team members to attend GDPR breakfast workshops. These are regularly held by law firms and associations such as the Association of Compliance Officers in Ireland (ACOI) and the International Association of Privacy Professionals (IAPP), with opportunities to attend around the country
3. Half-yearly or annual GDPR refresher courses. Again, there are many options, from one-day onsite workshops to online resources that can be accessed remotely at work or from home
4. Encouraging the team's data champion to join a data protection society, committee or working group, and reporting back the findings to the broader business unit
5. Circulating blogs and articles on GDPR hot topics such as data breaches, subject access requests and international data transfers.

[70] Carlos E. Perez, 'Natural stupidity is more dangerous than artificial intelligence', *Medium*, 14 October 2017, https://medium.com/intuitionmachine/natural-stupidity-is-more-dangerous-than-artificial-intelligence-1250a437cdb4

The Data Protection Commission runs a regular series of podcasts and posts useful advice and guidance on its website and social channels

6. Inviting data champions from other departments to present to the team. This can be extremely useful in understanding how colleagues have tackled similar challenges, and encourages sharing throughout the organisation. It can create what academic and author Carol Dweck refers to as a growth mindset[71] within the team and the business

At the very minimum, your marketers should undertake a GDPR refresher course annually. The team should also have a standing item for data privacy at its weekly meeting to keep it a live agenda item.

The Importance of Data Champions

According to Robert Half, 'When one teaches, two learn.'[72]

In any firm, there will be primary 'owners' of the data protection and compliance function. The data protection officer, head of compliance, chief privacy officer and director of corporate affairs are four examples. However, data protection must be owned throughout the organisation. Most businesses are too big to rely on oversight from a handful of privacy experts. It is the responsibility of everyone in the firm.

More than two years since the introduction of GDPR, too many staff in all manner of businesses still cling to ignorance or lack of knowledge as a reasonable response in the face of a data compliance breach. It is a worrisome trend.

One of the best ways to inculcate a data privacy mindset across your team, particularly in multinational and multi-departmental marketing teams, is to identify data champions. These will be frontline and middle management team members who demonstrate an interest or passion for data protection.

---

[71] Carol Dweck, *Mindset: Changing the way you think to fulfil your potential* (2017). The following YouTube talk gives a very useful overview of this important approach to learning: https://youtu.be/hiiEeMN7vbQ

[72] Nobel-prize-winning physicist Richard Feynman was another strong advocate of teaching as a way to truly embed what one has learned. His four-step learning technique included pretending one is teaching the topic or concept to a student in sixth grade (age 11 or 12).

Companies and institutions such as Eir and the University of Edinburgh have recognised the benefit of having champions throughout their organisation.[73] They act as the regular point of contact for individual departments and business units with the main data protection and compliance team. Consider who on your marketing team might suit such a role. Ideally, they should be detail-oriented, be willing to speak their mind and act as ongoing advocates for data privacy. If they attend training sessions or workshops, encourage them to share their insights with other team members. This could be as simple as circulating an email summary along with PowerPoint slides, or more structured through a mini-training session with the rest of the team.

Be Prepared to Iterate

The entrepreneur and lean start-up founder Steve Blank advised that 'no business plan survives the first contact with a consumer.'[74] Boxer Mike Tyson put it more succinctly: 'Everyone has a plan until they get punched in the mouth.' Both are takes on the truism that all strategies require adaptation once they meet the real world. Nothing ever goes quite as planned.

For marketers and data protection experts, it is a timely reminder. We spend considerable effort each year putting in place plans and strategies that will require constant amending and iteration once they are live in the marketplace.

Data protection training and development must be considered in the same manner. Experience over weeks, months and years will highlight aspects of team training that need strengthening, or particular risks that require more emphasis. The point is not to avoid planning, but to recognise that it is a continual project. Many businesses appear to have approached GDPR in an ad hoc manner. Significant expense was spent on training staff in the run-up to 25 May 2018, but how often has training taken place since then?

---

[73] University of Edinburgh, 'Data protection champions and steering group', https://www.ed.ac.uk/records-management/roles-responsibilities/data-protection-champions

[74] Steve Blank, 'No business plan survives first contact with a customer – the 5.2 billion dollar mistake', 1 November 2010, https://steveblank.com/2010/11/01/no-business-plan-survives-first-contact-with-a-customer-%E2%80%93-the-5-2-billion-dollar-mistake/

One of the unifying traits of the world's major belief systems is their recognition that men and women must be continually exposed to tenets and doctrines if they are to absorb them. Otherwise, a natural entropy sets in. While the analogy only stretches so far, training and development of your marketing team should take a similar approach in terms of structure and repetition. If data protection fails to be a living, breathing, daily part of your department's working day, it will atrophy. That is the point when the risk of breaches arising from human error increases exponentially.

TEDx speaker Matthew Syed talks about the importance of marginal gains to success in business and in life.[75] So, take the time to continually and iteratively build upon your data protection policies and procedures. Revisit them regularly to ensure they are effective and up to date. And for senior marketing leaders, remember that your actions set a very visible example to team members.

Use Checklists

Atul Gawande, in *The Checklist Manifesto*, describes the death of the master builder. In the modern world, it is not possible to be truly expert beyond a very limited number of subject areas. The master builder who would oversee every aspect of a construction in medieval and early modern times has been replaced by a range of experts with deep but narrow silos of knowledge.

We can learn from his advice when considering how marketers can best adopt data protection. He counsels on the importance of checklists. Simple but often overlooked, these lists can be consulted daily, weekly, or with regard to specific projects. Having a privacy checklist for your team is an ideal way to keep data principles to the fore. For instance, when the team considers a new way to share data, it might:

1. Review its existing data flows, based on the department's most recent audit
2. Assess whether a preliminary data protection assessment is required
3. Ensure that a third-party processing contract is in place where data is being shared with suppliers
4. Examine the existing legal basis for processing of the data

[75] Matthew Syed, 'Marginal gains', TEDx Talk, https://vimeo.com/337284728

5. Review current retention schedules for the data set
6. Review existing privacy notices relating to the data

This example is not intended to be comprehensive. Rather, it shows how such a structured approach can be beneficial for marketers. Having a system is usually the best way to achieve our goals. When it comes to data privacy, this rule still holds.

Keep Data Protection on Your Senior Leadership Team's Radar

If you are a team member or junior manager within a larger marketing function, it can be difficult to envisage how to promote a data protection culture. Such initiatives typically need senior level buy-in. One way to do this is to actively champion data protection with your line manager and colleagues; to act as a de facto data champion for the team, and encourage discussion and debate about the importance of data protection for marketing professionals as leading users of personal data within the business. I have seen how such an approach can slowly, iteratively develop a stronger understanding of the importance of privacy. The message can be both positive and negative – data is now one of the key resources of the twenty-first century, and those businesses that demonstrate a respectful approach to how data is used stand to benefit reputationally and in terms of customer goodwill.

This is important at a time when studies show a low level of trust among consumers. A 2018 report by the Chartered Institute of Marketing stated that only 34 per cent of 24- to 35-year-olds in the UK trusted businesses with their personal data.[76]

Understanding Data Protection Can Create Synergies

There is one further benefit that a strong training programme can provide. It relates to synergy. Howard Gardner, in his influential work *Five Minds for*

---

[76] Warwick Ashford, 'Businesses failing to win consumer trust', *Computer Weekly*, 27 November 2018, https://www.computerweekly.com/news/252453268/Businesses-failing-to-win-consumer-trust

the Future,[77] talks about the importance of the synthesising mind. The professional with this type of mindset is able to bring together disparate disciplines and learning, combining them in interesting and effective ways that benefit the business.

Having a team of marketers with a deep understanding of data privacy can create such synergies. Article 25 of the GDPR emphasises the need for data protection by design and default. Marketers who understand this principle can develop products, services and campaign strategies that effectively deliver their objectives while fully respecting consumer privacy.

As we head into a future of work that will be increasingly defined by advances in technology, artificial intelligence and machine learning, this synthesis of data principles and marketing techniques will prove invaluable to many firms. Just as a deep understanding of technology assists today's modern marketer, so in coming years will a thorough understanding of data privacy best practice provide advantages and career momentum to the next generation of marketing professionals.

Why This Is Important for Marketers

As we have seen throughout this book, the data protection landscape is becoming increasingly complex, particularly for marketers whose remit extends internationally. While marketers are responsible for large volumes of data within a business, it is fair to state that data protection has not typically been seen as a core function for the profession. This has to change. The downside risks of a data breach are sizeable, in terms of brand, reputation, financial impact and customer trust – all aspects of importance to marketing teams.

Human error is one factor, if not the main factor, in a majority of data breaches. Marketing teams that fail to undergo regular, systematic training in GDPR and data protection best practice significantly increase the risks to their business. Data privacy must be part of the team's culture. There is too much churn of staff in most marketing departments to rely on once-off or occasional training.

There are further benefits, too, in relation to the synergies that can be created when marketers fundamentally understand principles such as

[77] Howard Gardner, *Five Minds for the Future*, Harvard Business Review Press, 2009, https://howardgardner.com/five-minds-for-the-future/

data protection by design and default. In a rapidly changing environment, be prepared to iterate. Plans will undoubtedly require change in response to new technologies, legislation and marketing platform development. A well-trained team is one of the best ways you can ensure compliance with both the spirit and the letter of the law.

15

Looking to the Future: e-Privacy, Adtech and Machine Learning

Chapter 15 at a glance

1. Further data privacy laws are planned at EU level; these will impact on marketers.
2. Much of the momentum is due to the EU's commitment to a digital single market. This requires a solid privacy and data protection framework to ensure trust, commonality and transparency.
3. The ePrivacy Regulation (ePR) will result in significant changes regarding online communications, website cookies and direct marketing. It is currently the subject of significant lobbying at EU level.
4. Differences currently exist in how EU member states interpret best practice use of cookies on websites. Marketers with a presence in multiple European countries should refer to each local supervisory authority's guidelines. The Irish Data Protection Commission (DPC) issued new cookie guidelines in April 2020.

5. The adtech model appears profoundly flawed. A lack of transparency in how personal data is used and shared, and the potential for ad fraud, are drawing the attention of European regulators.
6. Artificial intelligence and machine learning will be defining technologies of the next decade. They present particular data privacy issues.
7. Ethics will be an important skill for marketers and business leaders as they distinguish between what can be done and what should be done.

The data privacy landscape extends beyond GDPR. As the EU seeks to develop a unified digital single market across member states, a range of laws that are planned and pending will impact on data protection. These will ensure that the EU's digital economy is built on a common foundation of transparency and trust.

In this chapter, we will look at some upcoming privacy legislation and how it will affect marketers. We will also consider the impact of increased data protection laws on the adtech model used by our industry, and the complexities that artificial intelligence (AI) and machine learning present for marketing and compliance professionals. We shall also explore the growing importance of ethics for marketers in the twenty-first-century economy.

e-Privacy: Present and Future

The EU is committed to a digital single market. First proposed in 2015, work has been ongoing over the past six years and across presidencies. One of the key pillars, alongside GDPR, is the ePrivacy Regulation (ePR). This seeks to update the Privacy and Electronic Communications Directive 2002 and subsequent amendments in 2009, known by many as the cookie law.[78] The new Regulation will provide more clarity on data protection regarding electronic communications, e-direct marketing and the use of website cookies. In doing so, it recognises the step change in

[78] A cookie is a small data file generated by a website and saved by your web browser. It is typically used by a website so that it can 'identify' the user, for example his or her previous purchase or viewing history on the site. The current Directive was adopted into Irish law by Statutory Instrument No. 336/2011. It is the reason a cookie consent form is presented when you first visit a site.

technology and services that has taken place since the Directive was first drafted.

Current e-privacy legislation is separate from but complementary to the GDPR. It is known as a *lex specialis* – a law governing a particular subject matter. The Data Protection Commission (DPC), which enforces e-privacy and GDPR in Ireland, advises that 'organisations must comply with both laws, but the rules under the ePrivacy legislation apply first when you are considering your organisation's use of cookies and other tracking technologies.'[79]

The current Directive states that a person shall not use an electronic communications network to store information, or to gain access to information already stored in the terminal equipment of a subscriber or user, unless:

1. The subscriber or user has given his or her consent to that use, and
2. The subscriber or user has been provided with clear and comprehensive information in accordance with the Data Protection Acts. This must be prominently displayed and easily accessible and includes, without limitation, the purposes of the processing of the information.[80]
3. The exception is for storage or access that is strictly necessary to provide the required service.

Proposed Changes under the New ePrivacy Regulation

At its core, the EU's proposed ePrivacy Regulation (ePR) seeks to ensure that providers of communication services handle data in a way that protects data subjects' privacy and rights, adhering to the principle of confidentiality. If introduced, ePR will affect marketers in a number of ways.

1. **Streamlining cookie rules.** The EU wishes to change current practices around website cookies, which many find annoying and ineffectual. Mirroring the GDPR principle of privacy by design and default, web browsers will be required under the ePR to provide users with a range

---

79 DPC, 'Guidance Note: Cookies and other tracking technologies', April 2020.

80 Ibid.

of cookie options and tracking controls. By default, these should provide the maximum level of privacy, with consumers having the ability to amend these if they wish to consent to increased tracking or profiling.

2. **Content and metadata.** The Regulation will guarantee the privacy of the content of a communication (e.g. voice, text, video and imagery). This also extends to the metadata associated with the communication. For example, data relating to location, the time it was sent, and information about the device that was used to send it.
3. **Electronic direct marketing.** Businesses will be prohibited from sending any unsolicited electronic direct mail, where consent has not been given. An opt-in will be required. The exception is where email details have been obtained in the context of a sale or service. Marketers should note that postal direct marketing falls outside ePR, but is within the scope of the GDPR.
4. **Telemarketing.** Most marketing teams still undertake some level of phone marketing. It's particularly important for business-to-business sales. Firms using this method will need to display their phone number or use a special prefix number that indicates that it is a marketing call.
5. **Legal persons are also covered.** GDPR is focused on 'living persons'. The ePR has a wider remit and includes businesses as 'legal persons'. If the ePR is implemented, companies will need to spend significant time and resources tracking and auditing the data flows of such communications. This includes machine-to-machine communications, an increasing element of society's move to an 'internet of things'.
6. **Tracking walls will no longer be permitted.** This is contentious, particularly for the advertising and publishing industries. If these articles are included in the final draft, it will stop companies requiring consumers to accept tracking in exchange for accessing online content. It poses challenges for the business models of media firms.
7. **Substantial fines.** Fines under the new Regulation will be at the same potential levels as GDPR, with a maximum fine of 4 per cent of global turnover or €20 million, whichever is the greater.

Originally intended to be introduced alongside GDPR, the Regulation has been affected by disagreements amongst EU member states as to its scope. Despite numerous drafts, the legislation is still undergoing amendments.[81] Current forecasts suggest that the Regulation is unlikely to be introduced before 2022. For the moment, the best policy is to adopt a 'watch and wait' approach. Ask your team's data champion to regularly monitor the progress of the legislation.

Unclear about Cookies

The delay in introducing the ePrivacy Regulation is causing problems for marketing teams who want to be compliant in their use of website cookies. As we have seen, the new Regulation will streamline the rules regarding their use. In the interim, marketers are faced with conflicting advice as to best practice.

Businesses with a multinational presence are especially affected. In Britain and Spain, consent must be given before a site activates analytics cookies (for example, tracking page views). This is not always the case in France or Germany, where a more nuanced approach is taken. The Irish authority advises that analytics, targeting and marketing cookies require consent, but notes that it is 'unlikely that first-party analytics cookies would be considered a priority for enforcement action'.[82]

Similarly, there are differences as to what counts as affirmative consent. The Spanish authority, for instance, recognises continuing to scroll or clicking a link on a web page as constituting such consent. France and Germany, however, do not view the continued use of a website as meeting this requirement.

Websites that present visitors with 'cookie walls', requiring consent before continuing to the main site, are deemed non-compliant in France and Germany, while the Information Commissioner's Office in the UK does not take a direct stance on the matter.

International companies must therefore take local guidance on best practice as pertaining to that country's supervisory authority. Despite Europe's best efforts at a unified approach to data privacy, there are still

81 Müge Fazlioglu, 'The GDPR, one year on: what about eprivacy?', IAPP, 29 May 2019, https://iapp.org/news/a/the-gdpr-one-year-on-what-about-eprivacy/

82 DPC, 'Report by the Data Protection Commission on the use of cookies and other tracking technologies', 6 April 2020, https://www.dataprotection.ie/sites/default/files/uploads/2020-04/Data%20Protection%20Commission%20cookies%20sweep%20REVISED%2015%20April%202020%20v.01.pdf

differences between member states, and these can be the cause of considerable headaches if interpreted incorrectly.[83]

New Cookie Guidelines from the DPC

In Ireland, the DPC issued new guidance on the use of website cookies in April 2020. It is highly recommended that Irish marketing teams take the time to review this document. Key points for marketers to note are:

1. The DPC provided a six-month 'grace period' for businesses to comply with its best practice guidelines. This commenced on 6 April 2020 and expired on 5 October 2020.
2. The guidelines apply to other tracking technologies as well as cookies, for example, pixel trackers, like buttons and social sharing tools, among others. Companies must be aware of any data that is being shared with third parties, for example through social tools. A 2019 decision by the European Court of Justice found that companies can be considered a data controller where such data is being shared.
3. The rules apply even where the cookies are not storing personal data. This is a useful distinction between ePR and GDPR. The former is focused on the confidentiality of communications. If personal data is stored, the additional requirements of GDPR apply.
4. Consent must be freely given, specific, informed and unambiguous.
5. Cookies deemed 'strictly necessary' for delivery of the service are exempt.
6. Analytics cookies will require consent. Marketers at multinational firms will need to bear in mind the variations in the interpretation of cookie laws across Europe.
7. Pre-ticked boxes and bundled consent, where approval is sought for a range of processing activities, are not allowed.
8. Consent must be reaffirmed every six months. The DPC views this as best practice. For digital marketing teams overseeing company websites, it will be important to work with your IT department and

[83] The IAPP provides a useful overview of the different interpretations among EU member states: Gabriel Voisin et al., 'ICO, CNIL, German and Spanish DPA revised cookies guidelines: convergence and divergence', IAPP, https://iapp.org/resources/article/ico-and-cnil-revised-cookie-guidelines-convergence-and-divergence/

relevant third-party suppliers (for example a consent management provider or CMP), to automate this process to ensure compliance.

9. Similarly, businesses must have clear retention periods for each cookie. Retaining cookie data indefinitely does not meet the GDPR's requirement for proportionality.
10. The guidelines do not recommend a particular method for obtaining consent. But recognise that website cookie banners are a typical way of achieving this objective.
11. Continuing to use a website or scrolling through the landing page does not imply consent. It must be an affirmative action by the consumer (for example, ticking a box). Similarly, a consumer is not deemed to have consented due to default settings on the browser they use.
12. Companies are recommended to have both a cookie policy and a privacy policy on their website, as these will meet the separate requirements of the ePR and the GDPR respectively.
13. Finally, every effort should be made to present the cookie banner information in a clear and accessible manner. This is particularly important for web users with visual impairments.

The Adtech Model Is Under Threat

Online advertising is big business. In Ireland, total spend in 2019 was estimated at €527 million, a 7.8 per cent increase year on year.[84] Media experts expected this to grow by a further 7.5 per cent in 2020 to €566.4 million. Facebook and Google dominate the market, with 81 per cent of online spend going to these two tech giants.

At a global level, digital advertising is forecast to reach $520 billion by 2023, an average annual growth rate of 15 per cent. Analysts expect Amazon to play an increasing role, with its ad revenues forecast to reach $40 billion that same year.[85] How the Covid-19 crisis accelerates and affects these long-term trends remains to be seen.

However, there are significant headwinds on the horizon for the industry. This is prompted by GDPR and growing consumer concerns

[84] Core, 'Outlook 20', https://onecore.ie/wp-content/uploads/2020/03/Core-Outlook-20.pdf

[85] Juniper Research, 'Digital ad spend to reach $520 billion by 2023, as Amazon disrupts Google & Facebook duopoly', 24 June 2019, https://www.juniperresearch.com/press/press-releases/digital-ad-spend-reach-520-billion-by-2023

around privacy and the use of personal data. The DPC recently reported a 75 per cent year-on-year increase in the number of data breach notifications it received. We have also seen large fines proposed in the UK and in Europe for alleged data breaches.

Regulators Have Online Advertising in Their Sights

Regulators appear to have the adtech industry in their sights. Over the past eighteen months, two of the largest European data protection authorities – the Information Commissioner's Office (ICO) in Britain and the Commission Nationale de l'Informatique et des Libertés (CNIL) in France – have outlined their plans for the sector.

On 20 June 2019, the ICO issued a report warning adtech to clean up its act. In doing so, it outlined several areas of concern regarding the use of personal data in real-time bidding for programmatic advertising. It highlighted issues around transparency, lack of clarity in privacy notices, the scale of data creation and sharing, and the reliance on contractual agreements within the supply chain. The report referenced a 'lack of maturity' among some participants in what was deemed an extremely complex marketplace involving multiple technologies.

Online advertising was a priority for the French supervisory authority in its action plan for 2019–2020. The CNIL also made the news for a €50 million fine issued to Google for breaches of GDPR. In the summer of 2019, it published guidelines on the use of online cookies and what constitutes consent on the part of the consumer. Stakeholders were given a grace period of twelve months within which to achieve compliance.

Ad Fraud

The issue of online fraud provides further complexity. Global ad fraud is estimated to cost the world's economy up to $30 billion per annum. A recent report by Cheq describes researchers as 'stunned by the scale of fraud in online advertising'.[86]

The direct cost to advertisers is forecast to reach $32 billion globally by 2022. Smaller firms may be disproportionately affected as they lack the resources necessary to prevent or combat fraud.

---

86 Cheq, *Ad Fraud 2020: The Economic Cost of Bad Actors on the Internet*, https://www.cheq.ai/adfraudcost

The industry is undertaking efforts to remedy the situation. However, the scale of the problem has generated significant concerns among global media buyers. According to Cheq, when Procter & Gamble reduced its digital spend by $200m, shifting that budget elsewhere, it subsequently increased its reach by 10 per cent. As author and Dilbert cartoonist Scott Adams advises, 'when lots of money and lots of complexity are in play, fraud is nearly guaranteed.'[87]

An unquestioning belief in online appears to be a factor. Author Bob Hoffman, a long-time critic of digital ad fraud and marketers' obsession with technology, has written that the 'addiction to targeting, which digital technology has amplified, has derailed the advertising industry from concentrating on its real job – creating more effective messages'.[88]

What Actions Can Marketers Take?

Senior marketers can take a number of steps to respond to these ongoing issues. First, with regard to cookies and consent, chief marketing officers (CMOs) and marketing leaders need to sit down with their legal and compliance teams to review the policies and procedures used on their company's websites. Useful steps include:

- Provide information on the use of cookies in a clear and transparent manner.
- Assess whether a customer could reasonably be expected to understand how their data will be retained, processed and shared with other parties.
- Undertake a full audit of partners and third-party sites with which customers' personal data is shared.
- Replace 'implied consent' mechanisms, such as pre-ticked boxes, with options that provide the consumer with the ability to clearly express their consent.
- Ensure that consumers have given their consent before non-essential cookies are activated.

---

[87] Scott Adams, *Loserthink: How Untrained Brains are Ruining America*, Portfolio, 2019.

[88] For an interesting read on marketing as a mix of art and science, check out *Quantum Advertising* by Bob Hoffman (2015). The author is insightful and hard-hitting in equal measure.

- Avoid the use of terms that 'nudge' behaviour. The ICO gives the example of pages that use words such as 'agree' or 'allow' versus non-compliant terms such as 'reject' or 'block'. This terminology nudges the consumer towards giving their consent.[89]
- Where multiple sites are used across EU member states, marketers need to ensure that local best practice advice from each country's supervisory authority is adhered to.

With regard to ad fraud, CMOs need to audit their current digital marketing spend and presence. Does the company have full clarity on the range of sites its programmatic creative is appearing on, or is it relying on agency assurances? Cybersecurity expert Dr Augustine Fou has highlighted the issue of moral hazard in an industry seeking expanding inventory for its clients while at the same time attempting to reduce ad fraud.

Looking more broadly at programmatic advertising, marketing heads should assess whether efficiency is being chased at the expense of effectiveness. Commentators such as Les Binet, Richard Shotton and Rory Sutherland have emphasised the importance of context and signalling. Marketers must weigh the return from targeting on potentially sub-premium sites with the longer-term brand-building benefits associated with placements on more reputable, top-tier platforms. Most important of all, look to work only with trusted partners and suppliers.

Automation and the Future of Work

Another complexity for marketers is the growth of machine learning and artificial intelligence (AI) technologies. These promise to have a profound impact on employment, productivity and the future of work. A study undertaken by the University of Oxford forecast that 47 per cent of jobs would disappear over the next 25 years,[90] while the McKinsey Global

---

[89] For more on nudge theory, cognitive biases and the factors that influence persuasion, see Thaler and Sunstein (2009), Kahneman (2011), Shotton (2018) and Cialdini (2007).

[90] Carl Benedikt Frey and Michael Osborne, Working Paper: 'The Future of Employment: How Susceptible Are Jobs to Computerisation?', Oxford Martin Programme on Technology and Employment, 17 September 2013, https://www.oxfordmartin.ox.ac.uk/downloads/academic/future-of-employment.pdf

Institute advises that almost every occupation has the potential for at least partial automation.

It is clear that the era of a single, career-long job is a thing of the past. Lifelong learning and a commitment to adaptable, transferable skills will be key in responding in an agile manner to the changing needs of the economy.

Governments recognise the potential that new technologies offer for economic growth. Significant changes are taking place at EU and national policy level. A new national cyber-security strategy was introduced by the Irish government in late 2019, as part of its commitment to deliver on the EU's digital single market strategy. Work is also at an advanced stage, as of late 2020, on a national artificial intelligence (AI) strategy.

The Importance of Ethics

When we look at the topic from the perspective of data protection, challenges emerge, for example how AI and machine learning can and should be used. Through big data, marketers have the potential to understand their customers and target markets at a level of granularity that is unprecedented. Merging data sets from a variety of consumer touch points can provide highly targeted profiling. Many big firms are hiring PhD graduates to join dedicated big data departments for this very purpose.

The question for marketers is how to balance the targeting and business benefits of these technologies with their broader moral and ethical responsibilities. In an era when brand purpose has never been so popular, it is more important than ever that a business ensures that it is ethically sound before showcasing its social consciousness and liberal credentials. Corporate social responsibility must extend beyond community initiatives and support for progressive legislation. Companies and marketing teams that fail to see the importance of sound data privacy principles will face significant reputational, trust and brand damage should their actions impact on an increasingly data-savvy public.

The public is wary but also weary. A study by Professor Joseph Turow[91] at the University of Pennsylvania highlighted that consumers view the obtaining and processing of their personal data by businesses with a

[91] Sapna Maheshwari, 'Sharing Data for Deals? More Like Watching It Go With a Sigh', *New York Times*, 24 December 2018, https://www.nytimes.com/2018/12/24/business/media/data-sharing-deals-privacy.html

sense of futility. They see no way to avoid the transaction. Turow states, 'people are very uncomfortable with surveillance but they don't know what to do.'

For this reason, ethics is likely to be an increasingly important component of modern business. Engineers can tell a business what can be achieved; but without a strong moral compass, it is easy for a company to misuse data. At a time when many senior marketers in Ireland are calling for a standardised and professional marketing education structure, there is a strong argument that ethics must form a core element of such training. Many professionals, such as accountants, lawyers and compliance experts, are mandated by their accrediting bodies to undertake annual ethics programmes as part of their continuous professional development (CPD). The Marketing Institute and other leading bodies must seriously consider how to build an ethics CPD component into any proposed education for our sector.

Case Study

Eamonn runs a custom bike shop based in Naas. His company has recently started selling online, in response to queries and increased demand from customers nationwide. Eamonn notices the same questions are repeatedly being asked by enquirers. Following a discussion with his IT manager, he decides to include a chatbot function on the shop's website. A data protection impact assessment (DPIA) indicates that risks to personal data are low to moderate. They can be largely offset through a series of mitigating actions which his IT manager will implement.

Eamonn then turns his attention to the cookie policy and consent platform on the website. Having recently reviewed the DPC's guidelines on website cookies, Eamonn is aware that chatbot functions are deemed to be non-essential. Customers will therefore have to opt in when arriving on the site. This will give affirmative consent that they wish the cookies that use the chatbot to be activated. Eamonn works hard to ensure the text on the cookie policy is clear and easily understood. He asks some friends and former customers to review the text and give him feedback. Again, consulting the DPC guidelines, he advises his IT manager to set the cookie retention period to a maximum of one month, which was the period indicated as reasonable and proportionate following completion of the DPIA.

Eamonn then gives the go-ahead to launch the new chatbot function. He makes a note to review its effectiveness and continued GDPR and ePrivacy compliance on a quarterly basis during year one of its operation.

Why This Is Important for Marketers

Technology, privacy legislation and customer awareness of data protection are all changing rapidly. In the coming years, we are likely to see a fundamental shift away from the use of cookie technology. Google has indicated that it will seek to block third-party cookies on its Chrome browser, adopting a phased approach as it seeks alternative solutions. This mirrors decisions already taken by Safari and Firefox browsers. The adtech sector is coming under increased scrutiny from supervisory authorities across Europe. What this will mean for popular advertising channels such as programmatic, which has grown very rapidly over the past decade, remains to be seen.

In addition, marketers will need to grapple with technologies such as artificial intelligence and machine learning as these become increasingly commonplace in our economy. Ethics will be key. What can be done must be balanced with what should be done. It promises to be an exciting and challenging time. Marketing teams without a solid understanding of data privacy laws will struggle to fully comprehend this new ecosystem.

16

Supervisory Authority: The Irish Data Protection Commission

Chapter 16 at a glance

1. The Data Protection Commission (DPC) is the Irish supervisory authority responsible for overseeing data protection and privacy laws in the Republic of Ireland.
2. The DPC is one of the most high-profile regulators in Europe, due to the large number of global tech companies with EU headquarters in Ireland.
3. The DPC's supervisory and corrective powers have increased under the GDPR and the Data Protection Act 2018.
4. Under the Irish Data Protection Act 2018, when the commission receives a complaint from a data subject it is mandated to initially seek an amicable resolution between the two parties.
5. In the case of multinational companies, the 'one-stop shop' mechanism allows for a lead supervisory authority to be appointed in the country where it has its 'main establishment'.
6. A number of large fines have now been applied by European data protection authorities. However, there remains a lack of clarity and consistency across member states.

The Data Protection Commission (DPC) is the Republic of Ireland's regulator responsible for overseeing the GDPR and other relevant data protection laws, such as the Irish ePrivacy Regulations (2011) and the Law Enforcement Directive. It acts as the main point of contact with the European Data Protection Board, the European Commission, and other supervisory authorities. Led by Helen Dixon, the DPC is one of the most high-profile authorities in Europe. This is because of the number of large technology firms that have a base in Ireland. For example, Facebook, Google, Twitter, Amazon and LinkedIn all have substantial Irish operations. Under the GDPR's 'one-stop shop' mechanism, businesses with a multinational presence will be primarily regulated by the authority where they have their 'main establishment'. As a result, regulatory decisions taken by Dixon and her colleagues in the DPC have significant impact across the whole of the EU.

Recent funding increases from the government have reflected this important role. The DPC's budget rose from €3.6 million in 2015 to €19.1 million in 2021.[92] Staffing has grown too. In 2020, the DPC had a total staff of 150; it is expected these numbers will increase further in the next few years.

The commission is mandated under the Data Protection Act 2018 to initially seek an amicable resolution when it receives complaints from individuals regarding a firm's use of their data. However, as a regulatory authority it also has significant powers to investigate and sanction businesses and individuals should they be found in breach of data protection laws. As marketing professionals, it is useful to have a good understanding of the role of the DPC and how our businesses may be required to interact with it. In this chapter, we will look at some of the key aspects of the commission.

Independence

In order to fulfil its role, the DPC must operate independently. A supervisory authority has to be able to act without undue influence from government or other stakeholders. Article 52 of GDPR states: 'Each supervisory

[92] Data Protection Commission, 'Statement on funding in 2021 Budget', https://www.dataprotection.ie/en/news-media/press-releases/data-protection-commission-statement-funding-2021-budget

authority shall act with complete independence in performing its tasks and exercising its powers in accordance with this Regulation.'

To ensure its independence, members of an authority are required by the GDPR to act with integrity, refrain from any action incompatible with their duties, and not to engage in any incompatible occupation, whether paid or unpaid.[93]

Recital 121 of the GDPR goes on to state that data protection authorities must have their own staff, chosen by the authority or an independent body. These should be 'subject to the exclusive direction of the member or members of the supervisory authority'.

Amicable Resolution

The Data Protection Act (DPA) 2018 and the GDPR mandate that, following a complaint from an individual, the Commission should initially seek an amicable resolution. Section 109(2) of the DPA 2018 states that 'The Commission, where it considers that there is a reasonable likelihood of the parties concerned reaching, within a reasonable time, an amicable resolution of the subject matter of the complaint, may take such steps as it considers appropriate to arrange or facilitate such an amicable resolution.'

This is typically the case where, following initial examination of the facts, it becomes clear that there may be a valid basis for the data subject's complaint. In these situations the DPC advises businesses to make an 'appropriate gesture' to help resolve the matter. Section 109(3) notes: 'Where the parties concerned reach an amicable resolution of the subject matter of the complaint, the complaint shall, from the date on which the amicable resolution is reached, be deemed to have been withdrawn by the complainant concerned.'

When done in a timely manner, this can often be sufficient to avoid the DPC exercising its formal powers under the Act. It therefore benefits companies to respond swiftly and have clear processes in place to be able to do so when such complaints are received. It is often the case that issues arise from a grievance that has not been addressed at an earlier, frontline stage in the company. For example, a customer care team that doesn't deal adequately with concerns raised by the individual; or a scenario where the person feels they have been poorly treated by the business. As one of the

[93] Recital 121, GDPR.

main points of interaction with a business, marketers should be mindful of any potential for such issues to escalate to the point where a complaint might be made to the DPC.

Corrective Powers and Sanctions

Articles 77–84 of the GDPR outline the corrective powers and sanctions available to the Commission. The DPC has the power to enforce a fine, remedial measures and other remedies from a data controller or processor. These are transposed from the GDPR into Irish law via Section 127 of the DPA 2018, and include:

1. Issuing a warning to a controller or processor.
2. Issuing a reprimand where data processing has infringed a relevant provision.
3. Ordering the controller or processor to comply with a data subject's request.
4. Ordering the controller or processor to bring processing into compliance, in a specified manner and within a specified period.
5. Levying a fine of up to €20 million or 4 per cent of global turnover, whichever is the greater
6. Ordering the controller to communicate a personal data breach to individuals
7. Imposing a temporary or definitive limitation, including a ban on processing
8. Imposing a restriction on processing
9. Ordering the suspension of data transfers to a recipient in a third country or to an international organisation
10. Serving an enforcement notice requiring the processor or controller to take such steps as the DPC considers necessary for the purposes of exercising one of the powers outlined above

In the case of a minor infringement or where a fine is likely to be a disproportionate burden on the business, the DPC may issue a reprimand instead.

Penalties and Fines

We have seen in earlier chapters that the potential for large fines has generated significant media coverage for GDPR. But how are these fines calculated? Article 83[94] outlines the criteria that must be taken into account:

> *(a) the nature, gravity and duration of the infringement taking into account the nature, scope or purpose of the processing concerned as well as the number of data subjects affected and the level of damage suffered by them;*
> *(b) the intentional or negligent character of the breach;*
> *(c) any action taken by the controller or processor to mitigate the damage suffered by data subjects;*
> *(d) the degree of responsibility of the controller or processor taking into account technical and organisational measures implemented;*
> *(e) any relevant previous infringements by the controller or processor;*
> *(f) the degree of co-operation with the supervisory authority;*
> *(g) the categories of personal data affected by the infringement;*
> *(h) the manner in which the infringement became known to the supervisory authority;*
> *(i) previous compliance with the DPC;*
> *(j) adherence to approved codes of conduct or other certification mechanisms;*
> *(k) any other aggravating or mitigating factor applicable to the circumstances of the case.*

Following a slow start, we are now witnessing the first substantial fines levied by EU data protection authorities under GDPR. In 2019, Britain's Information Commissioner's Office announced its intention to fine British Airways £183 million (€210 million) for a data breach affecting half a million of its customers; and Marriott International £99 million (€113 million) for a breach of nearly 340 million customer records.[95] In

[94] The full text of the Article can be found here: https://gdpr-info.eu/art-83-gdpr/

[95] As noted in an earlier chapter, the proposed fines were subsequently reduced to £20 million for British Airways and £18.4 million for Marriott.

March 2020, the Swedish authority fined Google nearly €7 million for not complying with the right to be forgotten. It is likely that this trend towards larger statement fines will continue over the next 24 months.

In May 2020, the DPC issue its first penalty to an Irish organisation under GDPR, with Tusla fined €75,000. Tusla received additional fines that year, totalling a further €125,000 relating to separate data breaches. In its most high-profile fine to date, the DPC penalised Twitter €450,000 in December 2020 for the company's handling of, and response to, a data breach.

There is still a lack of clarity among compliance and legal professionals as to how fines are being calculated. A consistent application has not yet emerged across EU member states. Further guidance would be particularly beneficial for firms with a presence in multiple EU countries.

Section 41(b) Requests from Law Enforcement

There may be occasions when your business receives a request from a law enforcement body for disclosure of an individual's personal data. Section 41(b) of the DPA 2018 allows a data controller operating in Ireland to disclose personal data where it is 'necessary and proportionate for the purposes of preventing, detecting, investigating or prosecuting criminal offences'.

Businesses in the insurance and banking sectors, for example, may regularly receive requests from An Garda Síochána for disclosure of customer personal data. It is natural to feel a responsibility to assist; however, it is important to note there is no obligation to comply if the request is made under Section 41(b). The risk is borne by the data controller. Where a decision is taken to do so, the business must ensure that, in its view, it is necessary and proportionate. A record should be kept, outlining the rationale for the decision. In the event that the company declines the request, law enforcement agencies have other routes open to them. For example, the Gardaí can request a search warrant from a district court, which then places a legal obligation on the firm to provide the information.

Context is key in such situations. Many businesses will choose to comply with a Section 41(b) request because they want to maintain a positive working relationship with police authorities.

Giving consideration, in advance, to how your business will deal with such issues is time well spent. Having a clear process, which includes feedback and input from key stakeholders in the firm, will ensure that any requests are responded to in a timely and thoughtful manner that respects GDPR best practice.

One-Stop Shop Mechanism

The GDPR introduced a new mechanism for multinational companies with a presence in a number of EU member states and that engage in cross-border processing. Under the one-stop shop, the supervisory authority where the company's main establishment is located will be the lead supervisory authority (LSA). The main establishment is the part of the organisation that largely or wholly determines the purposes and means of processing personal data.

There is some flexibility provided in the Regulation, where a case relates solely to data in one member state. Recital 127 advises that:

> ***Each supervisory authority not acting as the lead supervisory authority should be competent to handle local cases where the controller or processor is established in more than one Member State, but the subject matter of the specific processing concerns only processing carried out in a single Member State and involves only data subjects in that single Member State.***

Brexit will affect controllers or processors based in the UK who carry out cross-border processing of personal data across member state borders, but still within the EEA. The ICO provides a useful summary on its website regarding the potential impacts that these businesses should consider.[96]

Investigative and Auditing Powers

The Commission has a range of investigative powers at its disposal. These include: carrying out inspections; notifying an organisation of an alleged

96 ICO, 'EU regulatory oversight', https://ico.org.uk/for-organisations/dp-at-the-end-of-the-transition-period/data-protection-now-the-transition-period-has-ended/the-gdpr/eu-regulatory-oversight/

infringement; requesting information from the business; accessing a firm's records or entering its premises; and commissioning a report undertaken by a nominee of the DPC.

The DPC can also carry out an audit, by an authorised officer from the Commission, of your company's data processing activities, to ensure compliance with the GDPR and the Data Protection Acts 1988–2018. This can be held at very short notice and does not require a complaint to have been made. In some cases, it may be part of a larger review of a particular industry, where the DPC is seeking to ascertain general compliance levels across the sector.

The DPC's annual report is a useful reference document. It outlines the key priorities for the Commission and provides a wealth of case studies that give an insight into the types of data breach that are under investigation and issues of non-compliance that the DPC wishes to highlight. For non-compliance practitioners, it is a relatively accessible text. The case studies in the report are useful in highlighting potential risk areas for your business, and for getting a sense of how the DPC deals with particular categories of data breach.

Why This Is Important for Marketers

Most marketing teams will be familiar at some level with the DPC, either as a result of coverage regarding GDPR, or the high profile of its commissioner, Helen Dixon. Some may also have had direct interaction with the agency relating to a data breach or other privacy concerns.

Understanding the role of the DPC and its enforcement powers is important. As a large user of data within the company, marketers must be aware of the guidance and advice issued by the commission. Recognising its legal requirement to pursue an amicable resolution is also key. Working with affected individuals to seek such a resolution can benefit your brand's reputation and consumer trust in the organisation, and prevent more punitive action by the DPC.

The commission also issues many useful resources that are beneficial for marketers. Examples include frequent blog articles on a wide range of topics, and podcasts providing insight into aspects such as website cookie best practice. For those organisations with a nominated data champion within their marketing team, it is useful for that person to regularly monitor the news section of the DPC's website for the latest updates and guidance on GDPR-related matters.

17

How Will the GDPR Develop in the Future?

Chapter 17 at a glance

1. The GDPR contains a mechanism whereby it must be reviewed after its first two years of operation, and every four years from that point onwards.
2. The core focus is on the effectiveness of the cooperation and consistency mechanisms, and the transfer of data outside the EU.
3. It is possible that the European Commission will undertake a broader review of the Regulation.
4. There are currently gaps in a range of areas, particularly in the consistency with which the GDPR is applied across member states, but also in the transparency with which it is applied.
5. In the absence of a new ePrivacy Regulation, more work is required to align GDPR and e-privacy guidance. There are currently significant variations at a national level.

The GDPR must be reviewed after its first two years of operation, and then every four years. This is mandated under Article 97 of the Regulation. The review must focus on the effectiveness of data transfers outside the EU, and the efficacy of cooperation and consistency mechanisms. The European Commission may take the opportunity to undertake a broader review. This would be timely. There are a number of aspects of the Regulation that require additional clarification and guidelines, to increase consistency across EU countries and to provide further transparency as to how it is applied. This is mainly due to the structure of GDPR, which takes a principles-based approach to data protection. As a result, local supervisory authorities and the European Data Protection Board (EDPB) are required to 'fill in the gaps'. Alongside this will be a growing body of case law and interpretation by the courts. In this chapter, we will explore the topic of GDPR's future in more detail.

What Constitutes Personal Data?

We live in an era of automation and machine learning; and as technology becomes increasingly complex, many firms are faced with a challenge to identify what does and does not qualify as personal data. We saw in Chapter 2 that internet protocol (IP) addresses can in certain instances be deemed personal data. As businesses adopt technologies such as artificial intelligence and machine learning, it will become increasingly difficult to identify all the ways in which data sets can be combined to potentially identify an individual.

Fines

There is still a lack of clarity as to why particular fines are levied. These appear to vary from one EU country to another. While the GDPR lists the range of factors that must be taken into account when considering a fine, it is much less clear as to the amount that should be levied. Statement fines, such as proposed by Britain's Information Commissioner's Office in the case of Marriott International are one such example. Yet in other EU jurisdictions one can find cases where much lower penalties are applied. Examples include Tusla's recent €75,000 fine by the Data Protection Commission (DPC) for unauthorised disclosure of children's personal data, and Sweden issuing a (still substantial) €7 million penalty on Google for failing to implement the right to be forgotten. It is very difficult for firms with a multinational European presence to put in place contingencies to take account of the impact of potential data breaches.

It is likely that case law, and increasing guidance from the EDPB, will fill these gaps over time. For the moment, no clearly agreed structure or common practice is in place. The issue will therefore continue to exercise company boards and audit committees as they seek to implement appropriate risk management mechanisms.

Right of Access Requests

Receiving a right of access request from a customer or individual can be one of the most onerous tasks a marketing team faces under GDPR. Depending on the length of the relationship with the data subject, it can involve substantial time and resources tracing all relevant information. The time limit of one month (extended to three months in some cases) to respond means that such requests can quickly become very urgent.

But what information should be provided? There is very little clarity at present. Some firms include copies of everything they have on file, redacting irrelevant or third-party information. Others simply list the types of data that is held. The latter is a much more palatable and resource-light option for firms, but it is unclear whether this is best practice.

It is often made more difficult by the response of a data subject. Ideally, the exact nature of the information is outlined at the outset – the particular timelines or dates involved, and the nature of the content. For example, a job applicant may seek to ascertain what information the company holds regarding her application, made on such a date. Yet marketing and compliance teams will just as regularly receive a reply that the individual wishes to have 'any personal information that is currently on file' relating to them.

It is recommended that, whichever approach is applied, the firm should operate it consistently, and keep a watchful eye on any further guidelines emerging from either the DPC or the EDPB.

There is also a question mark over what constitutes a frivolous or vexatious request. Again, this will vary depending on the volume of personal data that is collated during the periods between each request, and also on the industry or sector where the firm operates.

Derogations at National Level

Under GDPR, there are a number of areas where each country has some latitude in how the Regulation is implemented. These are known as derogations. For example, the minimum age required for digital consent differs across countries, with Britain opting for thirteen years of age while Ireland chose a threshold of sixteen years. Adhering to these local compliance requirements requires country-specific knowledge, which limits the original intention for the GDPR to provide consistency across all its member states. Other examples include the appointment of a data protection officer. In Spain, controllers such as schools and insurance firms must appoint a DPO. A centralised guide would be extremely useful for marketers and compliance professionals operating across multiple EU jurisdictions.

Controllers and Processors

Many firms remain unsure as to what constitutes a joint controller. This has led to instances where businesses have used this descriptor incorrectly. More guidance, at a granular or sector-specific level, would be extremely helpful to ensure controllers meet their compliance requirements.

Similarly, there remains inconsistency in the controller–processor relationship. Article 28 of the GDPR sets out a requirement for written contracts between the two parties. Having a set of standard contractual clauses for processors would be helpful in eliminating the differences in interpretation across EU countries. In particular, what rights the controller has with regard to sub-processors, in the event that the main processor goes out of business or is made bankrupt.

Data Transfers Outside the EU

The Schrems II case significantly impacted data transfers to parties outside the EU. The European Court of Justice's decision resulted in the invalidation of the EU–US Privacy Shield agreement. It has also led to a significant overhaul of standard contractual clauses (SCCs) and the introduction of proposed supplementary measures that businesses must consider, where third countries are assessed to have data protection regimes not at the level required by the GDPR. Supplementary measures, in particular, will substantially increase the compliance burden on firms.

In the absence of approved codes of conduct or certification mechanisms, and the difficulty in implementing binding corporate rules for any but the largest multinational businesses, this may require a revisiting of certain aspects of GDPR. Businesses must have a reasonably straightforward way in which to achieve compliance, given the globalised nature of the modern economy. It will not be feasible or proportionate to expect all firms, particularly small and medium businesses, to undertake a detailed analysis of local privacy and compliance conditions within potential export markets outside the EU.

Aligning e-Privacy and GDPR Requirements

We have seen in earlier chapters that the requirements under the current ePrivacy Directive are not fully aligned with those of the GDPR. The proposed ePrivacy Regulation should hopefully resolve these issues; however, it is bogged down in lobbying at EU member state level. In the interim, it results in variations in how individual countries view aspects such as cookie banner consent – an area where the requirements of e-privacy and data protection overlap.

In an Irish context, the recent DPC guidelines on website cookies has been helpful, particularly for those businesses operating only within Ireland. For those with a presence in a number of EU countries, knowledge of local laws is still required in order to remain compliant.

The EDPB released updated guidance in May 2020 on the issue of consent. It highlighted, for example, that cookie walls and scrolling as a form of consent are both non-compliant under GDPR. Such guidelines are helpful as there are still divergent practices across countries such as Britain, Spain, France and Germany.

It will be interesting to see how legislators respond when reviewing GDPR. How the ePrivacy Regulation progresses, whether it will ever come to fruition, and its relationship with data protection laws will all impact the level of complexity marketers and their businesses face when trying to remain compliant.

Data Protection by Design and Default

Another aspect of GDPR that impacts marketers is the requirement for data protection to be designed into the early specifications of any project, and that the default settings for products and services respect consumers' privacy needs.

For new businesses and start-ups, this is challenging but eminently manageable. For large, established businesses, it can prove considerably more complex. Systems and processes have been built up over years or even decades. Product development, marketing and engineering teams have established ways of working. It can take an exponential effort for these businesses to pivot existing practices.

As GDPR becomes more established, it will be worth noting lawmakers' views on the effectiveness of data protection by design and default, and whether it has been truly embedded into the culture and mindset of European businesses or remains merely an ambition.

Why This Is Important For Marketers

There are many elements of GDPR that require further clarification, and we have only covered a handful in this short chapter. This is to be expected as the Regulation takes on the task of creating a harmonised environment across all EU member states. Alongside continuing variations at national and local level, and ongoing challenges to core mechanisms such as SCCs, the Regulation must cope with a rapidly changing technology environment. AI, machine learning and big data promise to be huge growth drivers for European and global economies over the coming decade. How to balance the need for economic growth with the issues around transparency and accountability that these technologies present will be a fundamental trial of GDPR's ability to adapt and remain relevant.

Another consideration which has emerged recently is how to cope with the challenges of increased remote working by Europe's labour force. The emergence of Covid-19 has rapidly transformed many workplaces and people's working lives. It is unlikely that we will return to the previous status quo. Businesses, economies and legislators must all cope with this fundamental change and the privacy questions it poses.

For marketing and compliance professionals, it promises to be an exciting and demanding time. Remaining up to date across all aspects of GDPR will require considerable effort. This is particularly the case for multinational teams, which must also cope with an increasingly complex global privacy environment as countries seek to adopt their own data protection laws.

18

Mental Models and Frameworks: A Useful Toolkit

Chapter 18 at a glance

1. Marketers have to deal with a very fast-moving business environment. Recognising this, it is important to carve out time to focus on GDPR and compliance with privacy laws.
2. Mental models are a useful tool to provide such focus. Frameworks such as the Eisenhower Matrix can help differentiate between urgent and important compliance tasks.
3. When applied to a data protection and compliance setting, understanding which elements of a GDPR strategy will deliver the most immediate and impactful results will help concentrate resources where they are most needed.

As I write these pages, the Irish and world economies appear in turmoil. The impact of the Covid-19 crisis has been of such magnitude that a significant recession is likely, alongside a substantial spike in unemployment. Businesses have moved into tactical mode, responding to the next urgent item on their to-do list. Little time is available to focus on long-term brand building and strategic activity.

We know from research by marketing experts Les Binet, Peter Field and others that this is the very time when brands should be investing in the future. The ability to capture increased share of voice while competitors turn off advertising can set a business on a higher growth trajectory once the economy returns to normal. Yet it is difficult for many marketing teams to maintain such a balanced approach, keeping long- and short-term objectives in mind simultaneously, and maintaining a 60:40 split between brand and tactical activations. Pressure from a range of stakeholders tends to make a difficult situation tougher.[97]

In a similar manner, data protection and compliance best practice can be supplanted by the requirement for business continuity. Attention is placed on damage limitation to revenue and lead generation. The potential for a data breach, in such circumstances, is significant.

One antidote is the use of mental models. These are frameworks that aid in decision-making. They are drawn from a wide range of disciplines and can allow marketers to critically assess a particular decision or choice that has to be made. The GDPR's adherence to privacy by design and by default are two examples of such models applied to the field of data protection. In this short chapter, we will look at some approaches that you and your team can apply that may help you keep a clear head and a focused eye on compliance requirements.

Using First Principles

First principles thinking has been used by many business and political leaders over the centuries. It involves cutting down to the core of a problem, getting to the fundamentals of an issue. This seems straightforward. In reality, most of us become bogged down in detail. Our attention can stray to very granular or minor aspects.

Elon Musk is a strong proponent of this approach. He applied first principles thinking to revolutionise commercial space travel. Musk realised he

[97] Balancing long and short-term objectives is a topic across multiple disciplines, reflecting a fundamental challenge in business and in life. It is also demonstrated in ongoing discussions in the field of governance, regarding the optimal balance between conformance and performance.

could source individual component parts required for rockets at a fraction of the price quoted by suppliers of the finished product. In reducing costs and improving affordability, he opened up space travel to a much wider potential audience.

A great way to use first principles is to ask five 'why' questions. This can have particular relevance in the case of a marketing project which might require a data protection impact assessment (DPIA). Before getting to that stage, look at your initial objectives and rationale for the project. Consider in particular how it will use personal data. Define the nature of the problem or issue, then ask 'why' five times. In the case of a new mobile application for your company, it may look something like the example below.

An online retail business is capturing large volumes of personal data about its customers, and is considering adding cookies on shopping preferences for visitors to its website. The marketing manager asks a number of 'why' questions in order to better understand and explain the rationale to stakeholders within the company.

Q: Why do we need to retain this information about our customers?

A: Because having data on their shopping preferences will allow the site to retain a 'wish list' of items they are considering buying in the future.

Q: Why do we need to keep a 'wish list'?

A: Because previous customer surveys have indicated this is a service they are seeking.

Q: Why is it important for customers?

A: Pre-loading the information reduces the time taken to make a purchase.

Q: Why is that beneficial?

A: Survey data shows customers are busy professionals; their time is a scarce resource. Having a faster shopping experience will help increase retention and improve user experience and word of mouth.

Q: Why do we need to obtain the data via cookies?

A: A website cookie is a cost-effective way for our business to obtain this data and has a minimal negative impact on the site's user experience.

In larger firms, where you will need to make the case to compliance, legal and the broader DPIA team, putting this mental effort in at the outset will be extremely beneficial. You will have more clarity and confidence that the reasons for the proposed data usage are sound. Note: this should not be used as a substitute for the legal requirement to conduct a DPIA.

The 3Cs and 4Cs Models

The 3Cs framework is familiar to marketers and business strategists. Originally created by Kenichi Ohmae, a management consultant, it allows a business to assess its position and relative strength vis-à-vis its competitors, and in terms of the value the customer is seeking.

A similar model could be applied to a compliance setting. There may be opportunities to identify ways in which your company can add value and strengthen its reputation for trust and transparency with customers and the broader public.

Start by considering the data protection rights and entitlements of customers and potential applicants, to assess the value and benefits they are seeking. Then look at how your main competitors are meeting these requirements. Finally, look at your company's strengths, weaknesses and its obligations as a data controller under the GDPR.

- **Customers:** What are the changing values or behaviours of the customer that your firm should take account of? Can existing products or services be re-imagined to meet increased consumer awareness of their data privacy rights, and concerns regarding data usage in the 'surveillance economy'?
- **Competitors:** What unique selling points or product/service advantages do your competitors have and how can you avoid directly competing on these aspects? Where are their core data privacy competencies as a business? What do their customers experience?
- **Company:** Are there existing ways in which your firm is more trustworthy or reputable with regard to data privacy that could be utilised for marketing and promotional purposes? For example, few or no data breaches, or the use of leading-edge technologies to ensure data is secure. Are there ways in which you could improve processes and procedures to make data protection a defining element of your business?

An interesting approach is to expand the 3Cs model by adding a fourth element to take account of the Data Protection Commission (DPC).

- Are there particular aspects of GDPR that the Commission has highlighted as a priority, either in its annual report or its strategic plan?
- Has the Commission released guidelines, a press release to media or given an indication that an industry, sector or specific aspect of GDPR will be under review in the coming months or years?
- Are there useful case studies on its website or in its annual report that indicate breaches relevant to your business sector?

Adding the strategic priorities of the DPC allows your business to look holistically at the broader privacy landscape, current and emerging trends. It avoids a scenario where you make decisions purely on conditions within your industry or sector.

The Eisenhower Matrix

Modern life appears to speed up each year. From a marketing perspective, there have never been more options for promoting our businesses. It can be difficult, unless conscious consideration is given to the problem, to carve out sufficient time for your team to focus on GDPR compliance. One useful way to achieve this is with an Eisenhower Matrix.

Its name comes from US President Dwight D. Eisenhower, who had two terms in office during the 1950s and prior to that was a celebrated World War II general. By definition, he was a very busy man. He faced a key question – how to separate the urgent tasks in his diary from those that were truly important. He wanted to avoid a situation where he was clearing his desk of immediate priorities, but had no time to focus on the long-term strategic projects that would make a real difference to the people he governed. To achieve this, he created a matrix with four areas – urgent and important; important but not urgent; urgent but not important; and finally, items that were neither urgent nor important.

Urgent and important items were dealt with immediately. These were key projects or deadlines that he could not afford to miss. Next, he looked at important but not urgent tasks. These might include strategic planning for new motorways, city construction or progressive laws. He set aside time in the coming weeks and months to give these sufficient attention to ensure they were progressing as planned. Next were urgent but not important items; these he sought to delegate to a member of his team.

Finally, he looked at items that were not important or urgent. These he would remove from his diary.

In the following table, we look at how marketers might apply the Eisenhower Matrix to a range of compliance activities they wish to undertake.

Do Now: *Important and urgent* · Responding to a customer access request within the one-month time limit under GDPR	**Do Later:** *Important but not urgent* · Data protection training and development for staff
Delegate/outsource: *Urgent but not important* · Posting a blog article or news release on data protection best practice on the company's intranet	**Eliminate:** *Not urgent or important* · Continually monitoring social media sites for the latest news on GDPR

The Pareto Principle

One of the best-known mental models, the Pareto Principle, was developed by Italian economist and polymath Vilfredo Pareto in the nineteenth century. Through his research, he recognised a repeated pattern whereby 80 per cent of the results were dependent on 20 per cent of the input. For example, Pareto noted that 80 per cent of the peas in his garden came from 20 per cent of the plants. The more widely he looked, the more he found similar effects.

Over the years, other researchers have applied the 80:20 model to their disciplines. In a business setting, management have noted that 80 per cent of their business unit's results come from the top 20 per cent of performers on the team.

Productivity expert Brian Tracy, the well-known author of *Eat that Frog!*, advises that applying the Pareto Principle can have significant benefits for the effectiveness of individuals and teams. This is achieved by focusing on the 20 per cent of a task that will deliver 80 per cent of the results.

Think about this from the perspective of your marketing team and how it can achieve compliance with GDPR. Are there specific elements that, if delivered upon, might complete much of the heavy lifting required? For example, investing time in properly training your team in the fundamentals of data protection best practice could significantly reduce the potential for breaches due to human error. Identifying a champion on the team could go a long way to keeping GDPR uppermost in the minds of their colleagues. And putting in place clear procedures and policies can aid in a consistent, documented and deliberate approach to tackling a wide range of requirements under the Regulation, for example ensuring a timely response in the event of a subject access request.

We all have finite resources at our disposal. Using Pareto's framework can help make sure we spend our time and effort most wisely.

Critical Mass

Critical mass is a term most of us hear quite regularly. It is defined in the Merriam-Webster dictionary as 'a size, number, or amount large enough to produce a particular result'. It has a particular meaning in physics, relating to the amount of material needed to create nuclear fission. However, in a business setting it indicates a tipping point, for example a company that achieves sufficient scale to be viable or even dominant in its market sector.

We can apply the concept of critical mass to GDPR. Namely, what is the level of activity and engagement with data protection within your team that will achieve compliance with the core tenets of the Regulation?

Make a checklist of the activities your marketing department, team or business unit will need to complete in order to achieve this tipping point. For example, a structured training programme for all staff, regular updates and briefings on compliance best practice across the organisation, and a data champion to provide regular internal communications on the topic to colleagues and peers.

Like a flywheel that is initially slow to turn, once momentum gathers you will find it comparatively easy to build on your early compliance efforts. Competencies will develop, structures and procedures will formalise, and what Carol Dweck refers to as a 'growth mindset' will be created.

Why This Is Important for Marketers

We are all faced with increasingly busy and disruptive working environments, particularly in the current Covid-19 crisis and its aftermath. Many of the certainties businesses and departments relied upon have been upended. The inclination to focus purely on tactical, immediate activity rather than on long-term strategy is substantial.

In such a climate, having mental models to guide one's decision-making is a crucial advantage. They provide the necessary structure and checks to avoid rash, impulsive or ill-considered decisions by your marketing team and the business overall.

When applied to a data protection and compliance setting, understanding which elements of a GDPR strategy to prioritise to deliver the most immediate and impactful results can save a company many days and weeks of unnecessary effort.

Conclusion

The world of data privacy is fast moving, not unlike the marketing sector. How fast can be seen in the changes that have taken place during the course of writing this book. A few examples make this clear. The EU–US Privacy Shield was invalidated during the course of 2020. This is a very significant issue for the thousands of European and American businesses that rely on Privacy Shield for transfers of international data between the two jurisdictions. The European Court of Justice's decision on Schrems II, which resulted in this outcome, has also significantly affected the use of standard contractual clauses (SCCs). Again, this has substantial ramifications for businesses who use this mechanism to transfer data outside the EU, in particular for the many small and medium-sized businesses (SMEs) that had planned to utilise SCCs when dealing with UK data processors post-Brexit.

Another significant change occurred in the area of website cookies and tracking technologies. The Data Protection Commission's (DPC) guidance, issued on 6 April 2020, will have a fundamental impact on Irish businesses in a number of ways. For marketing and sales teams, it will require the resetting of baseline metrics such as page views and web visits, as analytics cookies are deemed non-essential. Similarly, customer service departments using chatbots will need to rethink how they deal with customers who do not opt in to accept this functionality on their websites. The short grace period – six months – left little time for companies to consider how best to respond.

The most momentous change, however, has been the rapid uptake of remote working by companies globally, in response to the lockdowns imposed as a result of Covid-19. The world of work has changed fundamentally. Many of us now use technologies such as Zoom or Teams on a daily basis, or find ourselves accessing household laptops or mobiles to deal with work queries. It creates a whole new set of privacy challenges for companies and their staff, challenges that marketing and compliance teams are still seeking to fully understand. Few of us, if any, were familiar with terms such as 'Zoom-bombing' even a few months ago, while the phrase 'you're on mute' must be one of the most repeated terms of the past year.

These examples illustrate how widely data privacy affects our businesses and our lives. They are a timely reminder that data protection cannot sit within a silo. It cannot be the sole preserve of the data protection officer, compliance team or legal department. Privacy impacts us all. And with increasing consumer awareness and rapidly advancing digital technologies, it is here to stay.

It is worth remembering, too, that the GDPR is still in its infancy. Much remains to be clarified. In particular, a standard baseline for the imposition of fines would be extremely welcome. It would allow businesses to accurately prepare and assess the risk levels associated with various forms of data breach. This will be achieved through case law over the coming years.

The digital economy continues to develop at a fast pace, and with it arise new privacy challenges. Automation, big data and artificial intelligence will power the twenty-first-century economy. The Irish government recently launched a new national cyber-security strategy. This will be complemented by a similar strategy on artificial intelligence. Both are required for Ireland to play its part in the EU's commitment to a digital single market. As these technologies are implemented, further opportunities will present for marketers to promote our brands, products and services. Having a grounding in the key pillars of GDPR, its ambition and spirit, will help us navigate these challenges.

I hope that readers of this book will have gained not just an understanding of the legal requirements of GDPR and e-privacy, but also a practical sense of how they impact their businesses. My aim at the outset was to help guide marketers through some of the more complex and nuanced aspects of data protection by using case studies to give a sense of the challenges that firms of all sizes can face. I would urge marketers not to be put off by the legal terminology associated with GDPR.

Sometimes perfection is the enemy of sufficiency. Build your knowledge iteratively. Take some time each day, week or month to understand the key components of the Regulation – the principles and legal bases are a great place to start. Over time, you will see many of the same issues repeat themselves, for example how to deal with an access request or respond to a data breach. This continuous learning approach will ensure you are well versed in the particular implications data privacy holds for those of us within the marketing profession.

I wish you well on your learning journey.

Steven Roberts, February 2021

Useful Resources

The **Data Protection Commission** (DPC) website is a very useful starting point for marketers seeking to understand aspects of GDPR and Ireland's e-privacy laws. The content is written in a clear and easily understood form, with a minimum of legal jargon. The DPC also produces short guidance documents, blogs, podcasts and other social content.

https://www.dataprotection.ie/

The **UK Information Commissioner's Office** (ICO) has a superb website that is a great resource for marketers. It is one of the foremost data protection teams in Europe, albeit this may become of less relevance as Brexit takes hold. I find it extremely helpful, particularly for aspects that the Irish DPC's site may not have covered in sufficient detail. The site includes a range of free templates for everything from data protection impact assessments to legitimate interest assessments.

https://ico.org.uk/

The website of the **International Association of Privacy Professionals** (IAPP) is very useful for privacy and compliance practitioners, providing news on the latest data protection developments in Europe and globally.

https://iapp.org/

The **Association of Compliance Officers in Ireland** (ACOI) is Ireland's leading body for compliance professionals, with over 3,000 members. Its Certified Data Protection Officer (CDPO) designation is widely recognised as a high-quality qualification for those seeking to progress a career in data protection. The ACOI holds regular workshops and webinars on a range of data privacy-related topics.

https://www.acoi.ie/

References and Bibliography

Adams, S. (2019). *Loserthink: How Untrained Brains Are Ruining America*, New York: Portfolio.

Amer, K. and Noujaim, J. (2019). *The Great Hack*, Netflix.

Article 29 Working Party, 'Guidelines on data protection impact assessment (DPIA)', European Commission, 13 October 2017, https://ec.europa.eu/newsroom/article29/item-detail.cfm?item_id=611236.

Article 29 Working Party, 'Guidelines on data protection officers (DPOs)', European Commission, 30 October 2017, https://ec.europa.eu/newsroom/article29/item-detail.cfm?item_id=612048.

Ashford, W., 'Businesses failing to win consumer trust', *Computer Weekly*, 27 November 2018, https://www.computerweekly.com/news/252453268/Businesses-failing-to-win-consumer-trust.

Baden-Württemberg State Commissioner for Data Protection and Freedom of Information, 'LfDI Baden-Württemberg verhängt sein erstes Bußgeld in Deutschland nach der DS-GVO' ('LfDi Baden-Württemberg imposes its first fine in Germany under the GDPR'), 22 November 2018, https://www.baden-wuerttemberg.datenschutz.de/lfdi-baden-wuerttemberg-verhaengt-sein-erstes-bussgeld-in-deutschland-nach-der-ds-gvo/.

BBC News, 'British Airways faces record £183m fine for data breach', 8 July 2019, https://www.bbc.com/news/business-48905907.

Binet, L. and Field, P. (2013). *The Long and the Short of It: Balancing Short and Long-Term Marketing Strategies*, London: Institute of Practitioners in Advertising.

Binet, L. and Carter, S. (2018). *How Not to Plan: 66 Ways to Screw It Up*, Kibworth Beauchamp: Troubador Publishing.

Blank, S., 'No business plan survives first contact with a customer – the 5.2 billion dollar mistake', *SteveBlank.com*, 1 November 2010, https://steveblank.com/2010/11/01/no-business-plan-survives-first-contact-with-a-customer-%E2%80%93-the-5-2-billion-dollar-mistake/.

Brinker, S., 'Marketing technology landscape supergraphic (2019): Martech 5000 (actually 7,040)', *Chief Marketing Technologist Blog*, 4 April 2019, https://chiefmartec.com/2019/04/marketing-technology-landscape-supergraphic-2019/.

Cheq (2020). *Ad Fraud 2020: The Economic Cost of Bad Actors on the Internet*, https://www.cheq.ai/adfraudcost.

Cialdini, R. (2007). *Influence: The Psychology of Persuasion*, New York: HarperBusiness.

Clark, D. 'Total number of sales, marketing and related associate professionals in the United Kingdom (UK) from 2011 to 2020', *Statista*, 4 November 2020, https://www.statista.com/statistics/319805/number-of-sales-marketing-and-related-associate-professionals-in-the-uk/.

Clear, J. (2018). *Atomic Habits: An Easy and Proven Way to Build Good Habits and Break Bad Ones*, New York: Avery Publishing Group.

Commission Nationale de l'Informatique et des Libertés, 'Ciblage pulicitaire en ligne: quel plan d'action de la CNIL?' ('Online advertising targeting: what action plan for the CNIL?'), 28 June 2019, https://www.cnil.fr/fr/ciblage-publicitaire-en-ligne-quel-plan-daction-de-la-cnil.

Commission Nationale de l'Informatique et des Libertés, 'Privacy impact assessment', https://www.cnil.fr/en/privacy-impact-assessment-pia.

Core, 'Outlook 20', March 2020, https://onecore.ie/wp-content/uploads/2020/03/Core-Outlook-20.pdf.

Cox, E.N. (2016). 'Dealing with cyber threats', *Governance*, January 2016, Issue 259.

Cudderford-Jones, M., 'How small business are tackling GDPR', *Marketing Week*, 11 April 2018, https://www.marketingweek.com/gdpr-small-businesses/.

Deutsche Welle, 'East German Stasi had 189,000 informers, study says', https://www.dw.com/en/east-german-stasi-had-189000-informers-study-says/a-3184486-1.

DLA Piper, 'GDPR Data Breach Survey', January 2020.

Data Protection Commission, 'Anonymisation-Pseudonymisation', https://www.dataprotection.ie/en/dpc-guidance/anonymisation-pseudonymisation.

Data Protection Commission, 'Data Subject Access Requests – FAQ', https://www.dataprotection.ie/en/dpc-guidance/data-subject-access-requests-faq.

Data Protection Commission, 'Rules for electronic and direct marketing', https://www.dataprotection.ie/en/organisations/rules-electronic-and-direct-marketing.

Data Protection Commission, 'Guidance on appropriate qualifications for a Data Protection Officer (DPO)', https://www.dataprotection.ie/en/organisations/know-your-obligations/data-protection-officrs/guidance-appropriate-qualifications.

Data Protection Commission, 'Information Note: Data breach trends from the first year of the GDPR', October 2019, https://www.dataprotection.ie/sites/default/files/uploads/2019-10/Info%20Note_Data%20Breach%20Trends%202018-19_Oct19.pdf.

Data Protection Commission, 'Annual Report 1 January 2019 to 31 December 2019', 20 February 2020, https://www.dataprotection.ie/en/dpc-guidance/publications/annual-report/annual-report-1-january-2019-31.

Data Protection Commission, 'Does the GDPR really say that? – Attendee lists and name tags', 28 February 2020, https://www.dataprotection.ie/en/dpc-guidance/blogs/does-gdpr-really-say-attendee-lists-and-name-tags.

Data Protection Commission, 'Report by the Data Protection Commission on the use of cookies and other tracking technologies', 6 April 2020, https://www.dataprotection.ie/sites/default/files/uploads/2020-04/Data%20Protection%20Commission%20cookies%20sweep%20REVISED%2015%20April%202020%20v.01.pdf.

Data Protection Commission, 'Guidance Note: Cookies and other tracking technologies', April 2020, https://www.dataprotection.ie/sites/default/files/uploads/2020-04/Guidance%20note%20on%20cookies%20and%20other%20tracking%20technologies.pdf.

Data Protection Commission, 'DPC statement on CJEU decision', 16 July 2020, https://www.dataprotection.ie/en/news-media/press-releases/dpc-statement-cjeu-decision.

Data Protection Commission, 'Data Protection Commission statement on funding in 2021 Budget', 13 October 2020, https://www.dataprotection.ie/en/news-media/press-releases/data-protection-commission-statement-funding-2021-budget.

Dweck, C. (2017). *Mindset: Changing the Way You Think to Fulfil Your Potential*, updated edition, London: Robinson.

European Commission, 'Adequacy decisions', https://ec.europa.eu/info/law/law-topic/data-protection/international-dimension-data-protection/adequacy-decisions_en.

European Data Protection Board, 'EU–US Privacy Shield – Second Annual Joint Review', 22 January 2019, https://edpb.europa.eu/sites/edpb/files/files/file1/20190122edpb_2ndprivacyshieldreviewreport_final_en.pdf.

European Parliament and the Council of the European Union, *Directive 95/46/EC on the protection of individuals with regard to the processing of personal data and on the free movement of such data*, 24 October 1995, https://eur-lex.europa.eu/legal-content/EN/TXT/?uri=celex%3A31995L0046.

European Parliament and the Council of the European Union, *Directive 2002/58/EC concerning the processing of personal data and the protection of privacy in the electronic communications sector (Directive on privacy and electronic communications)*, 12 July 2002, https://eur-lex.europa.eu/legal-content/EN/TXT/HTML/?uri=CELEX:32002L0058.

European Parliament and the Council of the European Union, *Regulation (EU) 2016/679 of the European Parliament and of the Council of 27 April 2016 on the protection of natural persons with regard to the processing of personal data and on the free movement of such data, and repealing Directive 95/46/EC (General Data Protection Regulation) (Text with EEA relevance)*, 27 April 2016, http://data.europa.eu/eli/reg/2016/679/2016-05-04.

Evans, M., White, L. and Regan, J., 'Schrems II judgement due in July – what this might mean for your outsourcing deal', *Norton Rose Fulbright Data Protection Report*, 17 June 2020, https://www.dataprotectionreport.com/2020/06/schrems-ii-judgement-due-in-july-what-this-might-mean-for-your-outsourcing-deal/.

Farnam Street Blog, 'The Feynman Learning Technique', 22 February 2021, https://fs.blog/2021/02/feynman-learning-technique/.

Fazlioglu, M., 'The GDPR, one year on: what about eprivacy?', *IAPP*, 29 May 2019, https://iapp.org/news/a/the-gdpr-one-year-on-what-about-eprivacy/.

Feldwick, P. (2015). *The Anatomy of Humbug: How to Think Differently about Advertising*, Kibworth Beauchamp: Matador.

Financial Reporting Council (2018). *The UK Corporate Governance Code*. London: Financial Reporting Council.

Frey, C.B. and Osborne, M., 'The Future of Employment', working paper, Oxford Martin School, 17 September 2013, https://www.oxfordmartin.ox.ac.uk/downloads/academic/future-of-employment.pdf.

Gaddis, J. L. (2018). *On Grand Strategy*, London: Penguin.

Gardner, H. (2009). *Five Minds for the Future*, Boston, MA: Harvard Business Review Press.

Gawande, A. (2010). *The Checklist Manifesto: How to Get Things Right*, London: Picador.

Goodwin, D.K. (2019). *Leadership in Turbulent Times: Lessons from the Presidents*, London: Penguin.

Government of Ireland, *Data Protection Act 2018*, http://www.irishstatutebook.ie/eli/2018/act/7/enacted/en/html.

Government of Ireland, *S.I. No. 336/2011 – European Communities (Electronic Communications Networks and Services) (Privacy and Electronic Communications) Regulations 2011*, http://www.irishstatutebook.ie/eli/2011/si/336/.

Greene, R. (2012). *Mastery*, New York: Penguin Putnam.

Hamilton, P., 'Data commissioner to look for more staff and funding', *Irish Times*, 7 March 2019, https://www.irishtimes.com/business/technology/data-commissioner-to-look-for-more-staff-and-funding-1.3817791.

Harari, Y.N. (2016). *Homo Deus: A Brief History of Tomorrow*, London: Harvill Secker.

Heimes, R. and Pfeifle, S., 'Study: GDPR's global reach to require at least 75,000 DPOs worldwide', 9 November 2016, *IAPP*, https://iapp.org/news/a/study-gdprs-global-reach-to-require-at-least-75000-dpos-worldwide.

Hoffman, B. (2017). *Bad Men: How Advertising Went from a Minor Annoyance to a Major Menace*, San Francisco, CA: Type A Group.

Hoffman, B. (2015). *Quantum Advertising: A Brief Reflection on the Nature of Advertising*, Kindle.

International Association for Measurement and Evaluation of Communication (2020). *Barcelona Principles 3.0*.

Information Commissioner's Office, 'EU regulatory oversight', https://ico.org.uk/for-organisations/dp-at-the-end-of-the-transition-period/data-protection-now-the-transition-period-has-ended/the-gdpr/eu-regulatory-oversight/.

Information Commissioner's Office, 'How do we do a DPIA?', https://ico.org.uk/for-organisations/guide-to-data-protection/guide-to-the-general-data-protection-regulation-gdpr/data-protection-impact-assessments-dpias/how-do-we-do-a-dpia/#how2.

Information Commissioner's Office, 'Legitimate interests', https://ico.org.uk/for-organisations/guide-to-data-protection/guide-to-the-general-data-protection-regulation-gdpr/lawful-basis-for-processing/legitimate-interests/.

Information Commissioner's Office, 'Right of access', https://ico.org.uk/for-organisations/guide-to-data-protection/guide-to-the-general-data-protection-regulation-gdpr/individual-rights/right-of-access/.

Information Commissioner's Office, 'Sample DPIA template', https://ico.org.uk/media/about-the-ico/consultations/2258461/dpia-template-v04-post-comms-review-20180308.pdf.

Information Commissioner's Office, 'Security', https://ico.org.uk/for-organisations/guide-to-data-protection/guide-to-the-general-data-protection-regulation-gdpr/security/.

Information Commissioner's Office, 'Statement: Intention to fine Marriott International Inc. more than £99 million for data breach', 9 July 2019, https://ico.org.uk/about-the-ico/news-and-events/news-and-blogs/2019/07/statement-intention-to-fine-marriott-international-inc-more-than-99-million-under-gdpr-for-data-breach/.

International Association of Privacy Professionals, 'Data Retention Policy Checklist', https://iapp.org/resources/article/data-retention-policy-checklist/.

Jehl, L. and Friel, A., 'CCPA and GDPR Comparison Chart', *Practical Law*, 2018, https://iapp.org/media/pdf/resource_center/CCPA_GDPR_Chart_PracticalLaw_2019.pdf.

Juniper Research, 'Digital ad spend to reach $520 billion by 2023, as Amazon disrupts Google and Facebook duopoly', 24 June 2019, https://www.juniperresearch.com/press/press-releases/digital-ad-spend-reach-520-billion-by-2023.

Kahneman, D. (2011). *Thinking, Fast and Slow*, New York: Farrar, Straus & Giroux Inc.

Lawne, R., 'Subject access requests and the search for proportionality', *Fieldfisher*, 26 February 2020, https://www.fieldfisher.com/en/services/privacy-security-and-information/privacy-security-and-information-law-blog//subject-access-requests-and-the-search-for-proport.

Maheshwari, S., 'Sharing Data for Deals? More Like Watching It Go With a Sigh', *New York Times*, 24 December 2018, https://www.nytimes.com/2018/12/24/business/media/data-sharing-deals-privacy.html.

McDougall, S. 'Summary report of adtech Fact Finding Forum, held 6 March 2019', *Information Commissioner's Office*, March 2019, https://ico.org.uk/about-the-ico/research-and-reports/adtech-fact-finding-forum.

Newport, C. (2016). *Deep Work: Rules for Focused Success in a Distracted World*, London: Piatkus.

New York Times (2020). 'The Privacy Project', https://www.nytimes.com/series/new-york-times-privacy-project.

Parrish, S. (2019). *The Great Mental Models Volume 1: General Thinking Concepts*, Latticework Publishing Inc.

Parrish, S., 'Eisenhower Matrix: Master Productivity and Eliminate Noise', *Farnam Street Blog*, April 2013, https://fs.blog/2013/04/eisenhower-matrix/.

Perez, C.E., 'Natural stupidity is more dangerous than artificial intelligence', *Medium*, 14 October 2017, https://medium.com/intuitionmachine/natural-stupidity-is-more-dangerous-than-artificial-intelligence-1250a437cdb4.

Pfeffer, J. and Slancik, G. R. (2003). *The External Control of Organizations: A Resource Dependence Perspective*. Stanford, CA: Stanford University Press.

Ryan, J., 'Regulatory complaint concerning massive, web-wide data breach by Google and other "ad tech" companies under Europe's GDPR', *Brave*, 12 September 2018, https://brave.com/adtech-data-breach-complaint/.

Rudd v Bridle and another (Rev 1) [2019] EWHC 893, https://www.bailii.org/ew/cases/EWHC/QB/2019/893.html.

Shapiro, S.P. (2005). 'Agency Theory', *Annual Review of Sociology*, Vol. 31, pp. 263–284.

Sharp, B. (2010). *How Brands Grow: What Marketers Don't Know*, Melbourne, VA: Oxford University Press Australia.

Sher-Jan, M., 'Data indicates human error prevailing cause of breaches, incidents', *IAPP*, 26 June 2018, https://iapp.org/news/a/data-indicates-human-error-prevailing-cause-of-breaches-incidents/.

Shotton, R. (2018). *The Choice Factory: 25 Behavioural Biases that Influence What We Buy*, Petersfield: Harriman House Publishing.

Snijders, W. (2018). *Eat Your Greens*, Kibworth Beauchamp: Matador.

Spadafora, A., '90 percent of data breaches are caused by human error', *TechRadar*, 8 May 2018, https://www.techradar.com/news/90-percent-of-data-breaches-are-caused-by-human-error.

State of California Department of Justice (2018), *California Consumer Privacy Act*, https://oag.ca.gov/privacy/ccpa.

Syed, M., 'Marginal gains', *TEDx Talk*, https://vimeo.com/337284728.

Taleb, N.N. (2007). *The Black Swan: The Impact of the Highly Improbable*, London: Penguin.

Thaler, R.H. and Sunstein, C.R. (2009). *Nudge: Improving Decisions About Health, Wealth and Happiness*, London, New York: Penguin.

Tracy, B. (2007). *Eat That Frog! 21 Great Ways to Stop Procrastinating and Get More Done in Less Time*, San Francisco, CA: Berrett-Koehler Publishers.

Tricker, B. (2019). *Corporate Governance: Principles, Policies and Practices*, fourth edition, Oxford: Oxford University Press.

University of Edinburgh, 'Data protection champions and steering group', https://www.ed.ac.uk/records-management/roles-responsibilities/data-protection-champions.

Voisin, G., Boardman, R., Assion, S., Clark Nevola, C. and Sampedro, L., 'ICO, CNIL, German and Spanish DPA revised cookies guidelines: convergence and divergence', *IAPP*, https://iapp.org/resources/article/ico-and-cnil-revised-cookie-guidelines-convergence-and-divergence/.

Weinberg, G. and McCann, L. (2019). *Super Thinking: Upgrade Your Reasoning and Make Better Decisions with Mental Models*, London: Portfolio Penguin.

William Fry, 'Advisor to the CJEU in the Schrems II case finds standard contractual clauses remain valid', 20 December 2019, https://www.williamfry.com/newsandinsights/news-article/2019/12/20/advisor-to-the-cjeu-in-the-schrems-ii-case-finds-standard-contractual-clauses-remain-valid.

Zuboff, S. (2019). *The Age of Surveillance Capitalism: The Fight for a Human Future at the New Frontier of Power*, London: Profile Books.